GW01606296

130 NEW WINEMAKING RECIPES

A guide to the making of wines both from ingredients which are old favourites and from the many new ones which are now on the market

---

By C. J. J. BERRY
(Editor, "*The Amateur Winemaker*")

Published by
"The Amateur Winemaker" Publications Ltd.
Andover, Hants

Second Edition

14th Impression 1974
15th Impression 1975
16th Impression 1975
17th Impression 1976
18th Impression 1976
19th Impression 1977
20th Impression 1977

Printed in Great Britain by:
Standard Press (Andover) Ltd., South Street, Andover, Hants
Telephone Andover 2413

SBN 900841 21 4

Introducing this book . . .

THE "Amateur Winemaker's" book of tested recipes—"First Steps in Winemaking"—has been so enormously popular that there has been an insistent demand that other recipes which have appeared in the magazine since "First Steps" was published should also be made available in book form. This little book is the result.

It contains over 130 tried, reliable recipes, many of which cannot be found in any other publications; above all we would recommend the peach and the banana, elderberry and rosehip "variations upon a theme". For easy reference all wines are listed alphabetically by their principal ingredients; where there are two main ingredients they are cross-indexed.

Whilst in the main the recipes are supplementary to the 130 or so which appear in "First Steps in Winemaking", we have taken care also to include certain well-tried favourites which have stood the test of time. This book is therefore self-contained. The two books together, however, present a collection of recipes which is uniquely comprehensive and up-to-date.

This book will tell you all you need to know to start making wine successfully, and to produce some attractive and unusual wines, with the minimum of theory.

Many of the recipes are my own, many were originally compiled by Mr. C. Shave, the well-known Birmingham winemaker, and others by Mr. Bryan Acton, Mr. Peter Duncan, Mr. Humfrey Wakefield, and other winemaking friends. The cartoons are by Rex Royle, regular contributor to "The Amateur Winemaker".

We hope you will enjoy this book, and that many new and exciting wines will grace your cellar as a result of it.

C. J. J. BERRY

Background to Winemaking

Nowadays there is a great boom in home winemaking, and this is understandable because thousands of people are discovering for themselves the pleasures of an exciting and absorbing hobby, with a really enjoyable "end product", to use a current TV idiom.

Legally, the position is that you may make as much wine or beer as you like at home—and some enthusiasts make hundreds of gallons a year—*but not a drop of it must be sold.*

And making wine at home is *not* difficult, despite what some of the experts say. Most of the utensils can be found in any kitchen—a large saucepan or kettle for boiling (stainless steel, aluminium, or sound enamel ware, but not iron, brass or copper), a large crock or bowl (white, not lead, glaze) bottles and corks, and a wooden spoon.

Other items which will be found useful are glass 1-gallon bottles or jars, fermentation traps to keep the wine from contamination, a yard of rubber tubing for siphoning, a corking machine, a large plastic funnel for filtering (the larger the better) and, if you wish to go further into the "mysteries", a hydrometer to help calculate the strength of your wines. This is dealt with in detail in *First Steps in Winemaking* (80p).

Notice that your utensils, apart from the boiler and crock already mentioned, should be of glass, non-resinous wood (oak, ash or beech), plastic or white glaze pottery (lead glaze can lead to poisonous results).

CLEANLINESS

Everything must be kept scrupulously clean by the use of boiling water or baking in the oven, where possible, or by the use of a sterilising solution which can be used to rinse out bottles and apparatus. This is easily made by dissolving two Campden tablets and ½-oz. citric acid in a pint of water. (Campden tablets are merely fruit preserving tablets.)

Any wine consists of: 1, Flavouring; 2, Water; 3, Sugar; 4, Yeast; and 5 (hardest to obtain!), Time.

All that happens when yeast, a living organism, is putin to a sugary solution, is that it feeds upon the sugar, converting it roughly half to alcohol and half to carbon dioxide, by weight, so that one finishes up with a pleasantly-flavoured alcoholic drink.

We extract the flavour from fruits and vegetables by boiling them, by soaking them in cold water, or by a combination of the two (i.e. pouring boiling water on them and leaving them to soak). Or we can simply express the juice by means of a press or juice extractor, and add the required amount of water to it.

As regards sugar, one need only remember that 2½ lb. per gallon is required to produce a wine with sufficient alcohol to keep, 3 lb. will usually produce a strong wine, and more, up to 4 lb., will produce a wine correspondingly sweeter, since the excess sugar will not be converted to alcohol.

YEAST

There are many types of yeast. Some winemakers stick to baker's or brewer's yeast, but we would recommend either a good-quality wine yeast or a good granulated yeast. All will make wine, of varying quality, and usually the decision as to which type to use resolves itself into a matter of personal preference.

IN ALL THE FOLLOWING RECIPES USE ¾ OZ. BAKER'S OR BREWER'S YEAST PER 1 GALLON OF LIQUOR, OR 1 LEVEL TEASPOONFUL OF A GOOD GRANULATED YEAST. WITH WINE YEASTS FULL INSTRUCTIONS ARE SUPPLIED.

Beware of "No yeast" recipes. No liquor will work *without* yeast; it means that you are relying upon the natural yeast in the fruit, or, if you have killed that by the use of boiling water or sulphite, on any "wild" yeast which happens to be in the air . . . and the gamble may not come off.

NUTRIENT

Yeast nutrient can be used to "boost" the action of the yeast and is particularly recommended in flower, mead and other wines where the liquor is likely to be deficient in certain trace minerals. One can obtain nutrient ready made up, but most chemists will prepare it to this formula:

Tartaric acid, 80 grains; ammonium sulphate, 60 grains; magnesium sulphate, 8 grains; citric acid, 55 grains; potassium phosphate, 30 grains. This is for 1 gallon of mead or *two* gallons of wine.

The chief ingredient, it should be noted, is the acid, and if the nutrient is temporarily unobtainable, the juice of an ordinary lemon, or two or three short "squirts" from an artificial lemon, will be almost as beneficial.

The fermentation should be in two stages—the first vigorous one when the yeast is multiplying itself to the required level, and needs air for the process, and the secondary, quieter one, when it is converting sugar to alcohol, during which time air should be excluded; it is then that one should employ the modern device of a fermentation lock.

This will act as a barrier to the vinegar fly, and to the vinegar bacteria which are the winemaker's biggest enemies.

If they infect the wine it will turn to a peculiarly flavoured vinegar, fit only for the drain. In the early stages, therefore, the wine must also be kept closely covered.

WINEMAKING SUMMARISED

1. Extract flavour from ingredients by pressing, boiling or soaking in bowl or crock.
2. Add sugar and yeast and ferment for up to 10 days in a closely-covered bowl in a warm place (75–75° F.).
3. Strain off, put into fermentation bottle, and fit fermentation trap, filling to within an inch of bottom of cork. Temperature: about 60° F. This fermentation will be much softer and will proceed for some weeks, but eventually all bubbling will cease.
4. "Rack", i.e. siphon, the cleared wine off the "lees", or yeast deposit at the bottom of the jar. This should be repeated about a month later, and usually a third racking after a further three weeks is beneficial. By now the temperature should have been reduced to 60° F. and the wine should be quite stable, with no risk of explosions!
5. Bottle when wine is about six months old and cork securely. Bottles are then stored, on their sides preferably, in a room at about 55° F.

Do . . .

Keep things very clean.

Keep air away except during first few days, and even then keep brew closely covered.

Use fermentation trap for secondary fermentation.

Keep fermenting bottles full to within 1 in. of bottom of cork.

Strain wine well initially or it will be hard to clarify.

Keep a book and jot down all you do, so that you can repeat it.

Use new corks.

Keep red wines in dark bottles, to preserve their colour.

Don't . . .

Allow vinegar to get at brew.

Ferment in a metal vessel.

Put wine in old, damp bottles, or it may be infected.

Let sediment lie at bottom of bottle or it will impart a bad taste to the wine.

Rush a wine: give it time!

Forget to stir the "must" twice daily.

Use finings or filter unnecessarily; most wines will clear of their own accord, given time.

Use too much sugar, or your wines will be oversweet.

ALMOND (Calcavella) WINE

By Mrs. Maie Davis, of 4 Hampton Court, King's Lynn

Ingredients:

1 lb. raisins
3 lemons
3 lb. granulated sugar
Yeast and nutrient (she uses a Sauternes)
2 oz. almonds (sweet, a few bitter may be added)
1 gallon water

Method:

Chop the almonds and raisins and put them in muslin with the rind of the lemons. Boil gently. Add the sugar, stirring to dissolve, and the juice of lemons. Cool to blood heat and add yeast. Ferment 3–4 days, then strain into gallon jar to ferment, top up, and fit trap.

APPLE WINE

Apples make a truly delicious table wine, in the making of which there are only two difficulties—the pulping and the pressing. Cutting up large quantities of apples with a knife is a tedious and blister-making business and ideally the problem is solved by means of one of the neat apple mills or juice extractors that can now be obtained. Failing this, however, the job can be almost equally comfortably tackled with a chopping board and a small kindling chopper, holding it near the head and allowing the weight of the blade to do all the work. *Much* easier than a knife; the ancient Chinese knew a thing or two when they used heavy kitchen implements for chopping up food! A press for the pulp is a great help, but if you cannot buy, beg, or borrow one wrap your apple pulp in stout cloths, place the "pudding" on a strong open framework or laths (an iron footscraper or sieve) over a large vessel, and press upon it with your whole weight with your fists, and this will extract most of the juice.

The apples you use are important. The best eating apples do not make the best wine; usually the "rougher" the apple the better the result. Cider apples are ideal, cookers are a good second-best, and 1 lb. of crab apples in 10 will result in a great improvement. Russets are to be avoided, and a good plan is to use as big a mixture of types as possible.

If you have a real glut of apples use as much as 24 lb. to 1 gallon of water (the water will not cover them during mashing) and you will get a truly glorious wine; if you have fewer, use 12 lb. to the gallon and you will still get a delicious, but less full-bodied wine. The quantity can even be cut down to 6 lb. but the general opinion is that then the flavour and body are not wholly satisfactory.

Ingredients:

12–24 lb. mixed apples	**1 gallon water**
3 lb. white sugar to the gallon of liquor	**Yeast**

Method:

Chop or crush the apples into small pieces, put into a polythene bucket or dustbin, and add the water (cold) and two level teaspoons of a granulated yeast. Leave for about a week, closely covered, stirring vigorously from the bottom at least twice a day to bring the lower apple to the top. This system breaks all the accepted rules in that the fruit is not sterilised, either with boiling water, or with sulphite, yet we have never known the recipe to fail. Keep the bucket in a fairly warm place, of course. Then strain the juice from the pulp. Press the pulp as efficiently as you can and add the juice to the rest of the liquor. Measure, and for every gallon add 3 lb. of sugar. Put into cask or other fermenting vessel and fit fermentation lock, racking when it has cleared. The wine will probably be ready for drinking within six months, but is vastly improved by being matured in wood for a year. A further improvement can be effected by using a Sauternes yeast. If a really dry wine is required reduce the sugar by ½ lb.

APRICOT AND DATE

(See under Date and Apricot)

APRICOT SHERRY

Ingredients:

1 lb. dried apricots	**3 quarts water**
3½ lb. sugar	**Sherry yeast**
1 cup strong tea	**Yeast nutrient**

Method:

Wash the apricots well, and slice. Add three quarts of water and simmer for 30 minutes. Do not boil. Strain, add 3½ lb. of sugar and boil for a further five minutes. Add a breakfast cupful of strong tea and pour all into a gallon jar. Add the sherry culture or half-an-ounce of dried yeast, fit a fermentation lock in the neck of the jar, which should only be nine-tenths full, and set aside to ferment.

After a month empty the liquid from the fermentation lock, but lightly plug its upper end with cotton wool, and replace it, in order to give the sherry yeast the air it needs (if "ordinary" yeast is being used this is unnecessary).

Leave undisturbed for at least six months, then rack off into a clean jar, together with a little of the cleanest yeast from the bottom of the vessel and bring into a warm room

"Yes, you can make wine from almost ANYthing . . ."

for a few days to speed the final fermentation. When this has picked up remove vessel to a cool spot and leave for a further six months before bottling. When a year old, it is a most satisfactory sherry-flavoured wine.

BANANA WINE

Ingredients:

4 lb. peeled bananas
½ lb. banana skins
¼ lb. raisins
½ teaspoonful yeast
1 gallon water
1 lemon, 1 orange
3 lb. sugar

Method:

Use black or spotted bananas, whatever you can scrounge. Place bananas and fruit peel into a cloth bag and put the bag, tied up, into a large saucepan or boiler with the water. Bring to the boil, then gently simmer for half an hour. Pour the hot liquor over the sugar and fruit juice, and when the cloth bag has cooled squeeze it with the hands to extract as much liquor as possible. When all the liquor is lukewarm (70° F.) add the yeast. Leave it in a warm place for a week, stirring daily, then pour into a glass jar and move it to a cooler place; it will be a thick-looking mess, like a lot of soapsuds. Keep it well covered and in a couple of months it will have a large sediment at the bottom. Siphon off, then add the chopped raisins. Fit an air lock and siphon off again after four months; by then it will have started to clear. Leave a further six months before sampling. It improves the longer you keep it.

SPICED BANANA WINE

Ingredients:

3 lb. bananas (including skins) or 6 oz. dried variety
1 oz. cloves
1 oz. ginger
3½ lb. sugar
½ oz. citric acid (or 3 lemons no pith, in lieu)
1½ pints strong tea (a teaspoonful of grape tannin)
6 pints water
Yeast nutrient and activated wine yeast

Method:

Thinly slice the bananas and skins. Place these into the initial fermentation crock together with sugar, cloves and ginger, and pour in boiling water. Stir to dissolve the sugar and when cool add the citric acid and strong tea. Introduce the activated wine yeast and nutrient. Ferment on the fruit for 10 days, then strain into fermentation jar. Fit airlock and ferment to a finish in the normal way, racking as necessary in due course.

DRIED BANANAS

Ingredients:

12 oz. packet dried bananas
8 oz. raisins
2 teaspoons citric acid
2½ lb. sugar
1 gallon water
1 Vierka sherry yeast (Liquid or dry)

Method:

Simmer the dried bananas in the pressure cooker for 10 minutes. Make up the juice to 1 gallon with cold water. Add the raisins, citric acid and sugar. When quite cool add the yeast. Ferment on the pulp for seven days, stirring every day.

Strain into a gallon jar and ferment under the protection of a fermentation lock in the usual manner.

BANANA AND DRIED ELDERBERRY

Ingredients:

2 lb. bananas (including skins) or 4 oz. dried variety
1 lb. dried elderberries
3½ lb. sugar
½ oz. citric acid (or 3 lemons, no pith, in lieu)
½ pint cold strong tea (or a pinch of grape tannin)
7½ pints water
Yeast nutrient and activated wine yeast

Method:

Slice up thinly the bananas, including skins, and place into the initial fermentation crock, together with the dried elderberries and sugar. Pour in boiling water and stir until sugar is dissolved. When cool add the citric acid and strong tea. Introduce the yeast nutrient and activated wine yeast and leave to ferment on the fruit for 10 days, then siphon into fermentation bottles. Fit airlock, and leave to ferment in normal way, racking as necessary in due course.

BANANA AND FIG WINE

Ingredients:

2 lb. bananas (including skins) or 4 oz. dried variety
2 lb. dried figs
3½ lb. sugar
½ oz. citric acid (or 3 lemons, no pith, in lieu)
½ pint cold strong tea (or a pinch of grape tannin)
7½ pints water
Yeast nutrient and activated wine yeast

Method:

Chop the bananas and skins into small thin pieces. Similarly chop the dried figs and place these together with the sugar into a polythene bucket or crock vessel. Pour boiling water over the chopped fruit and then stir well. When cool add citric acid and strong tea; then introduce the yeast nutrient and activated wine yeast. Ferment on the pulp for 10 days, closely covered, then siphon in fermentation bottles. Fit airlock and allow to ferment in normal way. Rack as necessary in due course.

BANANA AND PARSNIP WINE

Ingredients:

2 lb. bananas (including skins) or 4 oz. dried variety
5 lb. parsnips
3½ lb. sugar
½ oz. citric acid (or 3 lemons, no pith, in lieu)
½ pint cold strong tea (or a pinch of grape tannin)
7½ pints water
Yeast nutrient and activated wine yeast

Method:

Scrub and thinly slice parsnips and boil slowly until tender, then pour the extract over the chopped bananas and skins. Add the sugar and stir until dissolved. When cool add the citric acid and strong tea, introduce the activated wine yeast and nutrient and ferment on the banana pulp for 10 days. Strain into fermentation vessels. Fit airlock and allow to ferment in the normal way, racking into clean jar when it clears.

BANANA AND PRUNE WINE

Ingredients:

2 lb. bananas (including skins) or 4 oz. dried variety
3 lb. sugar
2 lb. prunes
½ lb. raisins
½ oz. citric acid (or 3 lemons, no pilth, in lieu)
½ pint cold strong tea (or a pinch of grape tannin)
1 gallon water
Yeast nutrient and activated wine yeast

Method:

Thinly slice the bananas and skins, also slice in half the prunes, Place into the initial fermentation crock, add the chopped raisins and sugar. Pour in boiling water and stir until sugar is dissolved. When cool add the citric acid and strong tea. Introduce the yeast nutrient and activated wine yeast. Ferment on the pulp for 10 days, then strain into fermentation bottles. Fit air lock and leave to ferment in normal way, racking as necessary in due course.

BANANA AND RICE

Ingredients:

2 lb. bananas (including skins) or 4 oz. dried variety
3 lb. paddy rice (with husk)
½ lb. stoned raisins
3½ lb. sugar
½ oz. citric acid (or 3 lemons, no pith, in lieu)
½ pint cold strong tea or a pinch of grape tannin
7½ pints water
Yeast and nutrient

Method:

Place the finely chopped bananas and skins, paddy rice and stoned raisins, together with the sugar, into the initial fermentation crock. Pour in the boiling water and stir until sugar is dissolved. When cool add the citric acid and strong tea. Introduce the yeast nutrient and activated wine yeast and ferment for 10 days on the fruit. Then strain into fermentation jar. Fit airlock and ferment to completion in the normal way, racking as necessary in due course.

BANANA AND ROSE HIP SHELL WINE

Ingredients:

- 2 lb. bananas (including skins) or 4 oz. dried variety
- $\frac{1}{2}$ lb. dried rose hips or 4 oz. rose hip shells
- (A handful of Hawthorn berries (or more) or dried Elderberries will give this wine an excellent colour)
- $3\frac{1}{2}$ lb. sugar
- $\frac{1}{2}$ oz. citric acid (or 3 lemons, no pith, in lieu)
- $\frac{1}{2}$ pint strong cold tea (or a pinch of grape tannin)
- $7\frac{1}{2}$ pints water
- Yeast nutrient and activated wine yeast

"... and now may I introduce your Chairman ..."

Method:

Chop into thin slices the bananas and skins and pour over with boiling water. Add sugar and stir until dissolved. The rose hips, Hawthornberries and Elderberries, indeed all three if desired, should then be added. When cool add citric acid and cold tea. Introduce the yeast nutrient and activated wine yeast and ferment for 10 days on the pulp. Then strain into fermentation vessels. Fit air lock and ferment in the normal way, racking as necessary in due course.

DRIED BANANA AND ROSE HIP

Ingredients:

4 oz. rose hip shells
12 oz. dried bananas
1 gallon water
2 teaspoons citric acid
2½ lb. sugar
A Tokaier yeast

Method:

Bring half the water to the boil and pour over the rosehip shells. Simmer the dried bananas in the other half of the water in the pressure cooker for 10 minutes. Mix the two lots, add half a pint of cold water, and add the citric acid and sugar. Stir well. When cool (about 70° F.) add the yeast starter. Ferment on the pulp for seven days, stirring every day. Strain off into a gallon jar and ferment under a fermentation lock until clear, in the usual manner. Then siphon into a clean jar. Leave for a further three months before bottling.

BANANA AND SARSAPARILLA

Ingredients:

3 lb. bananas (including skins) or 6 oz. dried variety
2 oz. Sarsaparilla
3½ lb. sugar
½ oz. citric acid (or 3 lemons, no pith, in lieu)
1½ pints cold strong tea (or teaspoonful grape tannin)
7 pints water
Yeast nutrient and activated wine yeast

Method:

Thinly slice the bananas and skins and place into the initial fermentation vessel. Add the sugar and pour in boiling water. Stir to dissolve, then add the Sarsaparilla. When cool, add the citric acid and cold strong tea. Introduce the yeast nutrient and activated wine yeast. Ferment on the pulp for 10 days, then siphon into fermentation jars. Fit airlock and ferment to a finish in the normal way, racking as necessary in due course.

BARLEY
(and other grain wines)

Once the main rush of the winemaking season is over, why not make a good stock of a cereal wine? The usual favourites are barley, wheat or maize, although some like rice, and they can all be made from the same basic recipe, using 1 lb. of grain. Barley gives the smoothest wine, with most body, maize is intermediate in this respect, and wheat wine tends to be thinner and have more bite, and is often said to have a slight whisky flavour (although not, of course, whisky strength).

"Say if it's too strong for you . . ."

Ingredients:

1 lb. barley, maize or wheat
3 lb. white sugar
1 lb. raisins
2 lemons, 1 orange
Yeast nutrient
1 gallon water

Method:

Wash the grain, then soak it overnight in 1 pint of the water. The next day mince both grain and raisins in a domestic mincer (using the coarsest holes) and put into a crock or bowl with the sugar and the thinly-pared rinds of the fruit. Pour over them the remaining seven pints of water, boiling. Cover. Cool to 70° F. (tepid), then add the juice of the lemons and orange, the yeast, and yeast nutrient. Cover closely and leave in a warm place (65°–70° F.) for a week, stirring daily. Then strain into a fermenting jar and fit air lock; siphon off the lees when it clears, and refit lock. Leave for a further three months or so before racking into clean bottles.

When making rice wine use the above recipe, but use 3 lb. of rice instead of one.

BEERS AND STOUTS

MORGAN'S ALE

Ingredients:

1 lb. jar malt extract
½ lb. sugar
1 oz. hops (or to taste)
1 gallon water
Yeast

Method:

Boil up the ingredients in ½ gallon of water in pressure cooker for 30 minutes. Strain, add half a gallon of cold water, and yeast. Set aside to ferment, closely covered, and skim off the "cap" every 24 hours. When fermentation has apparently ceased (usually about a week), bottle in beer bottles, adding a level teaspoon of sugar to each bottle. Cork tightly and tie corks down, if not using screw stoppers. Stand in a cool place to clear. The beer is usually ready to drink after another seven days.

BERRYBREW
(a strong bitter)

Ingredients:

4 lb. malt extract	**1 teaspoon citric acid**
4 lb. sugar	**2 teaspoons salt**
4 oz. hops	**4–5 gallons water**
1 dessertspoonful Crosse and Blackwell's gravy browning	**Yeast**

Method:

Put hops (if preferred in muslin bag), salt and gravy browning (which is only caramel colouring) into some or all of the water (I use two gallons), but make sure you have a few extra hops to add later. Bring to the boil. Simmer for 40 minutes.

Add a few loose hops, simmer for a further five minutes.

Meanwhile stand the jars of malt extract in hot water for 10 minutes to facilitate pouring; then put the malt extract

"... he does an awful lot of wine judging . . ."

and sugar into a polythene bin and strain the hopped wort on to them. Stir well to dissolve, and add the acid. Make up to the desired quantity with the remainder of the water (2–3 gallons) cold. (If using a carboy for fermentation the whole of the wort thus prepared can be poured into it when cool.)

Allow to cool to 70° F., and then add a good brewer's yeast and nutrient. Use proprietary yeasts in quantities recommended, with baker's yeast use 2 oz., creamed in some of the wort, with granulated yeast, use 3 *level* teaspoons. Close the bin with a polythene sheet secured with elastic (or, if carboy, with air lock). Fermentation should be vigorous in 36 hours, complete in 10 days.

When the surface of the beer has cleared, and only tiny bubbles are visible in a ring in the centre (the gravity *must* be 1010 or below, and preferably down to 1000–1002) bottle in strong 1-quart beer or cider flagons. Fill to within 1½ inches of bottom of stopper, add *one level teaspoon* of white sugar to each bottle (not more!) and screw down hard. Put the beer in a cool (not cold) place and it will be clear and ready for drinking within a fortnight or less.

BOYS' BITTER

Ingredients:

1 lb. malt extract	**1 gallon water**
1 oz. hops	**Yeast**

Method:

This is an excellent basic beer, and its bitterness can be adjusted by increasing or decreasing the amount of hops proportionately. Since it is ready to drink after just over a week, you can experiment with two or three consecutive gallons and get the flavour to your personal taste before multiplying the quantities to make the beer in bulk. Whilst experimenting, pay regard principally to flavour, rather than to clarity, for to obtain complete clarity it is necessary to store the beer in a cool place for a month.

Bring the water to the boil, add the malt extract and hops, and simmer for an hour and a half. "Top up" to the original volume with more water, then strain through muslin into a large jug. (If you use normal one-gallon fermentation jars they must not be filled beyond the shoulder, because of the froth, so use an additional half-gallon one as well).

Add your yeast, and keep in a warm place (70° F.) for four days. Then siphon the beer off the yeast deposit into strong bottles. Add a cube of sugar to each bottle, and tie down the cork. (It is best not to use screw stoppers until you have really mastered the art of brewing; a tied-down cork will always give warning of impending disaster; a screw-stopper will not!). Move the beer into a cool place; it will be drinkable in another week.

OATMEAL STOUT

Ingredients:

- ¾ lb. rye
- ½ lb. black malt
- ½ lb. pale malt
- 6 oz. oatmeal
- 2 oz. hops
- 4 lb. sugar
- 4 gallons water

"Can't think where that judge has got to."

Method:

Crack the pale malt (but not the black) with a rolling pin and put all the malt into just under two gallons of water at 150° F. (60° C.) in a two-gallon bucket. Then insert a 50-watt glass immersion heater (costing about 37½p, such as is used in tropical fish tanks), wrap the bucket in a blanket or thick cloth, and leave the heater switched on for a period of eight hours; this can conveniently be done overnight. This will maintain the brew at the ideal temperature for mashing (65° C. or 150° F.) and extraction will be first-rate. Then pour into a boiler and add the hops, rye and oatmeal, and boil for an hour, adding a few extra hops in the last five minutes. Strain into the fermenting vessel on to the sugar and make up to just over four gallons with cold water. Cool to 75° F. before adding the yeast and fermenting in the usual way. When the surface of the wort begins to clear and bubbles are collecting centrally (or when the S.G. is nearing 1001) bottle, adding one level teaspoon of sugar to each quart, screw-stoppered bottle. Store in a cool, dark place until the homebrew clears, and pour out carefully and steadily to avoid disturbing sediment.

If you cannot obtain an immersion heater to do the extraction properly, all the ingredients (except, of course, the yeast) can be simmered in all, or some, of the water, the sugar added, and the wort then fermented, but the resultant "stout" will not be of quite such high quality.

SEWARD ALE

(to make 5 gallons)

Ingredients:

5 gallons water
Yeast
1½ lb. brown sugar
1½ oz. crushed barley
1¾ lb. brown malt extract
3 oz. hops

Method:

Soak the barley in a little water overnight and run it through a mincer. Boil the hops (the packeted variety will do), malt (obtainable from most *Amateur Winemaker* advertisers or [in 1 or 2 lb. jars] from the chemist) and barley for 30 minutes, in two gallons of the water. Strain on to the sugar and stir to dissolve it, then add the remaining three gallons of water (cold). Allow to cool to about 70° F., then add yeast, a good beer yeast or a level teaspoon of granulated yeast. Cover closely and allow to ferment in a warm place for 48 hours, skimming frequently. By then the S.G. should have dropped to about 1010. Bottle without disturbing the sediment, by using a siphon tube. Keep the beer another five or six days in a cool place, after which it can be drunk, but it will be vastly improved for being left another three weeks. If a darker beer is required (this one is light in colour) add up to ½ oz. liquorice to the five gallons.

BEETROOT WINE

Ingredients:

1 gallon water
4 lb. young beetroot
3 lb. sugar
Yeast
1 lemon
4 to 6 cloves
½ oz. root ginger

"And these are two I keep for my personal use . . ."

This recipe uses young beetroot, and the secret is to make sure that they are not overboiled.

Method:

Wash the beetroot thoroughly, then slice thinly. Bring to the boil in the gallon of water, with the thinly peeled rind of the lemon, the cloves and the ginger. Simmer until the beetroot is tender and loses its colour. Strain on to the sugar, preferably in a large bowl. Stir well to dissolve and when lukewarm (70° F.) add the juice of the lemon and the yeast (a pre-prepared wine yeast, a level teaspoonful of granulated yeast or ½ oz. baker's yeast). Cover and leave in a warm place (65–70) for two days to begin fermentation. Then pour into fermenting vessel and fit fermentation trap. Siphon off when it clears, and bottle when stable in dark bottles to preserve its colour.

BEETROOT AND PARSNIP WINE

(by C. Shave)

Ingredients:

2 lb. frosted parsnips
3 lb. old beetroot
4 lb. sugar
½ pint strong tea
1 gallon water
2 lemons
2 oranges or ½ oz. citric acid
Yeast nutrient
Yeast (selected wine or General Purpose)

Method:

Wash the roots well (do not peel), slice thinly and place in the gallon of water with the grated peel (no white pith) of the fruit, and the tea. Simmer until the roots are tender. (N.B.—Any overboiling may result in a cloudy wine). Strain and dissolve the sugar in the liquor and thereafter continue as for beetroot wine.

BEET AND PINEAPPLE WINE

. . . an unusual combination, but, having tasted it, we can vouch for the fact that it makes an excellent wine. The recipe is that of Mrs. M. Paton, of Muirend, Stewarton, Kilmarnock, Ayrshire.

Ingredients:

4 lb. beet	1 lb. raisins
1 large or 2 small pineapples	3 lb. sugar
2 lemons	1 gallon water
	Yeast

Method:

Wash the beet, but do not peel them, and cut into small pieces. Peel pineapples thickly. Put peel of pineapples and cut-up beet into pan, cover with the water, and boil till beet is tender, but not mushy. (The remainder of the pineapples can be eaten). Put sugar, raisins (washed and chopped) and sliced lemons into crock, and strain the hot liquor over them, stirring to dissolve the sugar. Allow to cool to 70° F., then add the yeast (and, preferably, some nutrient for it), cover with a thick cloth, and stand in a warm place to ferment. After five days or so, strain into fermenting jar and fit trap.

"That last lot of beer seems extra gassy!"

Rack off and bottle when wine has completely cleared. If after a while it throws a sediment, rack again. As an alternative, use just 3 lb. beet and 1 lb. black grapes. Crush the grapes and add them to the sugar, raisins, etc., in the crock. Use dark bottles.

BILBERRY (See Elderberry, p. 52)

BILBERRY Dried (See Elderberry, Dried, p. 57)

BLACKBERRY WINE (1)

Ingredients:

3 lb. blackberries	**1 gallon water**
3 lb. sugar	**Yeast and nutrient**

Method:

Pick the blackberries when they are fully ripe, and use only those of the best quality. Crush them in a bowl with a wooden spoon and add the water, mixing thoroughly. Allow them to stand overnight, then strain them through a nylon sieve on to the sugar, and stir well to dissolve. Add yeast and nutrient, cover closely with a sheet of polythene or thick cloth, and leave in a warm place (70–75° F.) for a week; then, when the first vigorous ferment has subsided, stir, and transfer to fermenting jar. Fit fermentation lock and place in a temperature of 60–65° F. for the main fermentation. If possible use an opaque coloured jar but if you have only a white or clear glass one, wrap it in brown paper or keep it away from the light, to preserve the wine's glorious ruby colour. Rack for the first time after three months, refitting air lock, and again into clean coloured bottles when the wine is finished (about two months later).

BLACKBERRY WINE (2)

Ingredients:

6 lb. blackberries	**1 gallon water**
3½ lb. sugar	**Yeast**

Method:

Wash the berries thoroughly in a colander, then crush them in a bowl and pour over them the water, boiling. Allow them to steep for two days, then strain the liquor through a nylon sieve on to the sugar, stir well to dissolve, and add the yeast. Pour into fermenting jar, filling to shoulder, and fit trap, and thereafter continue as usual. This makes a full-bodied, sweet, wine.

BLACKCURRANT WINE

Ingredients:

3 lb. blackcurrants
7 pints water
Yeast and nutrient
2½ lb. sugar

Method:

Strip any stems from the fruit and wash it well, crush in a bowl with a wooden spoon, and then proceed as for cherry and blackberry wines.

This makes a pleasant, dry and fairly light table wine. A wine with greater body and correspondingly greater sweetness can be made by increasing the weight of fruit up to 1 gallon (still with 1 gallon of water) and by adding 3½ lb. sugar to every gallon of the resultant liquor.

In this case pour *all* the water, boiling, over the crushed fruit, allow to stand for 24 hours, then strain off the liquor and measure it. Add 3½ lb. sugar to every gallon and then ferment, rack and bottle as above.

BROOM
(See Cowslip)

BULLACE WINE

Bullaces, or bullace plums, are seen in some gardens, and grow wild in many parts of the country, particularly in the Midlands, but many winemakers, seeing them for the first time, wonder what they are, although rightly sensing that they will make excellent wine. The best description one can give of them is that they are a cross between a plum and a sloe, both in size and appearance.

Ingredients:

4 lb. bullaces	**Yeast**
3 lb. sugar	**Yeast nutrient**
½ lb. raisins	**1 gallon water**

Method:

Crush the fruit to a pulp with a piece of hardwood and pour over it the water, boiling. Cover with a cloth and leave for five days, stirring once or twice a day. Strain through a nylon sieve, pressing with a wooden spoon to express as much juice as possible, and dissolve the sugar in it. Chop the raisins, put them in a colander, and pour some boiling water over them to sterilise them, then place them in a wide necked fermentation vessel. Add the liquor, the yeast nutrient, and your chosen yeast, cover the mouth of the jar with a sheet of polythene secured with a rubber band, and leave in a temperature of 65–70° F. When the wine has cleared appreciably and a deposit of yeast has appeared (about two months, usually) strain into fresh jar or bottle and fit fermentation trap. Rack once more after a further three months, and bottle. Use opaque or dark glass vessels throughout so that the wine will retain its colour.

CABBAGE WINE

(by C. Shave)

Ingredients:

2 lb. cabbage, including stalks
3 oranges or lemons ($\frac{1}{2}$ oz. citric acid may be used in lieu)
3$\frac{1}{2}$ lb. sugar
1 lb. crushed wheat, rice or barley
$\frac{1}{2}$ lb. minced raisins (scalded)
$\frac{1}{2}$ pint cold tea
1 gallon water
Activated yeast and nutrient

Method:

Mince the cabbage (including stalks) together with the grains (which have been soaked overnight), the scalded raisins and rinds (no pith) from the fruit. Place in fermentation vessel and add sugar, add the boiling water and stir to dissolve the sugar. When cool add the cold tea, fruit juices (or citric acid), activated yeast and nutrient. Ferment for 7 days, then strain into glass jar. Fit fermentation lock, ferment and rack in the normal way.

CARUM CARVI WINE

(Caraway Seed and Tea)

Ingredients:

1 oz. packet Caraway Seed
1 lb. raisins (or 1 pint grape concentrate)
½ oz. citric acid (or 3 lemons, no pith, in lieu)
3 lb. sugar
6 pints tea or thereabouts to produce 1 gallon must
Yeast nutrient and activated wine yeast

Method:

Add the Caraway Seed to a saucepan of boiling water and bring this to the boil with the object of extracting the flavour from the seed. Strain over sugar and stir until dissolved. Chop the raisins and after scalding add to the sugared caraway solution. When cool add the citric acid, cold tea, and introduce the yeast nutrient and activated wine yeast. Ferment on the pulp for seven days, then strain into fermenting vessel and ferment under airlock until it clears, then rack for the first time. Bottle when completely clear, about 3/4 months later.

This is a winner!

CARVI FRUCTUS

Ingredients:

1 oz. caraway seeds (Boots the Chemists)
1 lb. crushed barley, wheat or maize
2 lb. green gooseberries or stoned raisins
½ oz. citric acid or 3 lemons (no pith)
½ pint cold strong tea
3–4 lb. sugar
1 gallon water
Yeast nutrient
Activated yeast

Method:

Pour boiling water over the Caraway seeds, crushed grains, and sugar. Stir well to dissolve the sugar, then add the crushed fruit. When cool add strong tea, citric acid, nutrient and activated yeast. Ferment on solids for 7–10 days, stirring well each day then strain into fermentation glass jar. Fit air-lock and ferment to a finish and rack in the usual way.

CARNATION WINE

Ingredients:

- **2 quarts white "pinks"**
- **1 gallon water**
- **3 lb. sugar**
- **1 orange**
- **1 lemon**
- **½ lb. raisins**
- **Yeast, yeast nutrient**

"Got quite a kick, hasn't it?"

Method:

The delightful scent of these flowers does carry over into the wine and give it a really attractive bouquet which will particularly appeal to ladies (most men seem to prefer less "scented" wines). And it is easy to make . . . put the flower heads into a crock and pour over them the water, boiling. Leave for not more than three days, giving an occasional stir. Then strain, and squeeze out the flowers lightly. Chop the raisins and slice the fruit thinly, and add them, with the sugar and yeast nutrient, to the liquor. Stir well to dissolve the sugar. Finally, add your yeast, a wine yeast or a level teaspoon of granulated yeast. Ferment in a temperature of 65–70° F. for 10 days, keeping your pan closely covered, then strain into a fermenting bottle and fit air-lock. When the wine clears and there is a firm yeast sediment, rack into a clean jar, and keep for another three months, this time corked, before the final bottling. It will be usable after about four months in bottle.

CARROT WINE

Ingredients:

4 lb. carrots **1 gallon water**
3 lb. granulated sugar **½ oz. hops**
Yeast and nutrient

Method:

Scrub the carrots well and chop them up. Put them in the water, bring to the boil, and simmer until tender. Strain the liquid into another saucepan or boiler (throw away or eat the carrots!), and add the sugar and hops. Stir well to dissolve the sugar and just bring the liquor to the boil. Allow to cool. Strain into a bowl or through a nylon sieve or butter muslin, and when the temperature has dropped to about 70° F. add yeast, preferably a pre-activated wine yeast, and some yeast nutrient to "give it a boost." If you are using a one-gallon jar do not fill right up to the bottom of the neck in case the fermentation proves too vigorous; keep a little of the liquor aside in a milk bottle plugged with cotton wool. Keep the jar in a warm place, with an air lock fitted, and after five or six days the ferment will have quietened and it can be topped right from the bottle. Leave until the wine is clearing and a sediment has formed, then siphon it off the lees. Repeat this two to three months later when the wine is completely clear, and bottle.

CHAMOMILE WINE
(Anthemis nobilis)

Ingredients:

Chamomile Flowers (18 or so)
4 lb. carrots (swede or turnip if desired)
½ oz. citric acid (or 3 lemons, no pith, in lieu)
3½ lb. sugar
½ pint cold strong tea (or a pinch of grape tannin)
Sufficient water for 1 gallon must
Yeast nutrient and activated wine yeast

"Perhaps just a LEETLE too acid!"

Method:

Scrub the roots but do not peel. Slice thinly into cold water and boil until tender and strain on to sugar. Stir until dissolved. Pour boiling water on chamomile flowers and steep, as making tea. Add the strained infusion to the sugared root juice, also when cool add the citric acid, cold tea, yeast nutrient and activated wine yeast. Ferment under an air lock until it clears, then rack for the first time. Bottle when completely clear, about 3/4 months later.

A ¼ oz. grated Candied Angelica may be added if desired.

CHERRY WINE (1)

Ingredients:

8 lb. black cherries (weighed whole)	**3½ lb. granulated sugar**
	1 Campden tablet
7 pints water	**Yeast and nutrient**

Method:

Weigh the cherries whole, then remove stems, wash and stone fruit. Crush the cherries in a bowl, bring 4 pints of the water to the boil and pour over them. Cover closely with a sheet of polythene secured by elastic, or with a thick cloth, and leave for 24 hours. Then strain the liquor through a nylon sieve, or two thicknesses of muslin, and throw away the pulp, after pressing out as much juice as possible. Bring the other three pints of water to the boil and dissolve the sugar in it, then add this syrup to the liquid already obtained. When the whole has cooled to 70° F. (just tepid) add the yeast and nutrient and leave in a bowl or polythene bucket for 10 days, closely covered as before, in a warm place (65–70° F.). Transfer it then to a 1-gallon fermenting jar, topping up to the bottom of the neck if necessary with cold boiled water, and fit fermentation lock. Leave until all fermentation has ceased, then rack into clean jar. Rack again into bottles about two months later. A delicious, medium-sweet dessert wine.

CHERRY WINE (2)

Ingredients:

8 lb. sweet cherries (either black or red)	**Yeast**
	Yeast nutrient
2½ lb. white sugar	**1 gallon water**

Method:

Use only ripe fruit, and avoid any which is mouldy or damaged, or it may spoil the wine. Wash the fruit, chop it, place it in a bowl, and pour the cold water over it. Add the Campden tablet and allow the fruit to steep (well covered) for four days. Then place the sugar in a bowl or crock and strain the juice on to it, either through a nylon sieve, or through a jellybag or heavy cloth, squeezing well to express all possible juice. Stir well to dissolve the sugar, then add the yeast and yeast nutrient and pour into fermenting vessel. Ferment and rack in the usual way. Cherry wine made in this way will not have the deepness of colour that is obtained by extracting the juice by using heat, but it will have an

"But I only showed him round'

infinitely better flavour, that of the fresh fruit, and additional colour can easily be added, if desired, to the finished wine by using a little fresh red fruit juice or purchased cherry colouring.

CHRISTMAS DRINKS

OLD-TIME PUNCH
(10 wine glasses)

Ingredients:

1 bottle of any red wine	**Little grated nutmeg**
1 cup granulated sugar	**1 pint hot water**
1 level tablespoon honey	**2 sliced oranges**
1 lemon	**1 carefully peeled red apple**

Method:

Heat wine with sugar, honey, sliced lemon rounds and grated nutmeg in pan to near boiling point. Add the hot water. Pour over sliced orange and apple rounds in large bowl.

Decorate with whole length of apple peel.

SPICED CIDER COMFORTER
(8 wine glasses)

Ingredients:

3 level tablespoons honey	**Small stick cinnamon**
1 bottle vintage cider	**1 lemon**

Method:

Dissolve honey gently in cider over low heat, add cinnamon, lemon peel and juice. Serve hot.

WINE CUP

Ingredients:

1 bottle red country wine	**¼ pint gin**
1 lemon (juice only)	**½ pint sherry**
	1 siphon soda water

Method:

Mix all the ingredients together, garnish with slices of cucumber and a sprig of mint, and if desired enrich with candied cherries and a little maraschino. The cup should be served roughly at room temperature and should not be allowed to stand longer than unavoidable.

CHE-NA-GRUM

In Cornwall at Christmastide a favourite drink is Che-na-grum, or She-nac-rum—hot, sweetened beer flavoured with rum, grated nutmeg and sometimes ginger, and garnished with slices of lemon.

Method:

Place two lumps of sugar in a tumbler. Add a wine-glass of rum. Fill up the glass with hot boiled beer and float two slices of lemon on top. (Enough for one person)

WASSAIL BOWL

Ingredients:

3 pints ale	½ grated nutmeg
½ lb. brown sugar	Pinch of ground cinnamon
½ bottle sherry or Madeira	2 lumps of sugar
6 roasted apples	1 washed lemon
½ oz. ground ginger	½ lemon

Method:

Prepare the apples first. Core them, stuff with brown sugar, and roast in a covered dish for 20 minutes, then uncover, baste, and finish cooking. Mix the spices with the sugar. Place in an enamel saucepan; add 1 pint ale. Stir over low heat till dissolved, then bring to boil, draw pan to side of stove. Stir in remainder of ale, the sherry or Madeira, and the sugar, rubbed on to the lemon until all the oil is extracted. Heat till piping hot, but do not allow to boil. Pour into a hot, ornamental bowl. Add the hot, roasted, stuffed apples, then the half lemon, peeled so that all the white pith has been removed, and cut in slices. Place the bowl on a cake board or salver, and ornament round the base with holly or mistletoe. Serve at once with a ladle.

ALE PUNCH

Ingredients:

2 oz. castor sugar	½ pint sherry
1 lemon	6 ice blocks
2 quarts light ale	

Method:

Place the sugar in a punch bowl. Wash the lemon. Remove rind as thinly as possible and add to sugar. Extract lemon juice and strain over the sugar. Stand for ½ hour, then remove lemon rind. Add ale, sherry and ice. Garnish with 1 or 2 slices of lemon. Enough for 6 or 7 persons.

CIDER (Spiced)

(See Christmas Drinks)

CLARY WINE

This is a favourite wine in many parts of the country, and is made from the blue flowers of Clary Sage. Clary is a member of the sage family, and the blue blossoms are gathered if possible just before they show signs of deteriorating, which is generally in late summer. (Beekeepers: the Clary Sage is reputed to be a good "bee" plant and is a useful source of nectar as well as pollen). This recipe will make a medium-sweet, delicate wine.

Ingredients:

3 pints Clary sage blossom (or 1 pkt. Heath and Heather dried blossom)	**1 lb. raisins**
	2 lemons
	Yeast; yeast nutrient
3 lb. sugar	**1 gallon water**

"No thanks; I have my own"

Method:

If you are using the dried blossoms obtained from a herbalist it will be necessary to infuse for 24 hours before use. Boil the sugar in the water for a few minutes and ensure that it is all well dissolved, then pour the hot liquor over the clary blossoms, the chopped raisins, and the juice and thin rinds (no pith) of the lemons. When the temperature has dropped to 70° F. add the yeast, a wine yeast or a level teaspoon of granulated yeast, and some yeast nutrient. Cover closely and stand in a warm place for a week to ferment. After that period, remove the flowers, but leave the raisins in the liquor for a further 10 days before straining into a fermenting jar and fitting trap. Rack the wine for the first time when the top half is clear, and again about two months later when it has cleared completely.

COFFEE WINE
(by W. Beavis, Southend)

Ingredients:

½ lb. coffee
3 lb. sugar
2 lemons
1 gallon water
Yeast and nutrient

Method:

Peel the lemons thinly, avoiding the white pith (a grater is the ideal way) and boil the peel in the water with the coffee for half an hour. Strain on to the sugar and stir well to dissolve, allow to cool, and add the yeast, nutrient, and strained juice of the lemons. Cover closely and leave in a temperature of 65°–70° F. for about a week, before transferring to a 1-gallon fermenting jar and fitting air lock. Top up with cold boiled water or syrup if necessary. Leave to ferment right out, then transfer to a cool place (55 –60° F.) and siphon off the lees into clean bottles when it is completely clear.

COLTSFOOT
(See Cowslip)

FRUIT JUICE CONCENTRATES

Several readers have asked for recipes for using some of the fruit juice concentrates now available, so here are some they may care to try:

CIDER or PERRY (5 gallons): (S.G. 60). Use 1 gallon Concentrated Apple or Pear Juice. Use a reliable yeast nutrient, Steinberg, Champagne, All-purpose, Kaltgarhefe, or Perlschaum Yeast.

LIGHT APPLE or PEAR WINE (S.G. 100) (5 gallons): Use 1 gallon Concentrated Apple or Pear Juice, 3 gallons water and 5 lb. 6 oz. sugar dissolved initially in 5 pints water. Use a good yeast nutrient and Perlschaum, Rudesheimer, Tokay, All-Purpose or Cold Fermentation Yeast.

HEAVY SWEET APPLE or PEAR WINE (S.G. 150): 1 gallon of concentrated apple or pear juice plus 2½ gallons

"Just a little YOUNG, perhaps?"

of water. Make first a syrup by dissolving 12 lb. of sugar in 6 pints of the water. Add one-third of this syrup to the must and ferment with Sauternes, Tokay, All-Purpose or Sherry Yeast with a good nutrient. Add the remainder of the syrup in two doses at suitable intervals, when the fermentation slows. To make a gallon adjust ingredients accordingly.

CYSER ("Melomel"): Substitute 1 pint apple juice, concentrate for 1 lb. honey per gallon in any mead recipe and reduce any added acid recommended by at least ¼ oz. per gallon.

RHUBARB AND APPLE: Substitute 1 pint concentrate for 1 lb. of sugar per gallon in any rhubarb recipe and reduce any added acid recommended by at least ¼ oz. per gallon.

COWSLIP, PRIMROSE, COLTSFOOT, BROOM

The same basic recipe can be used for each of these wines, and the most important single point to note is that it is essential, if a wine of good strength is required, to use yeast nutrient. Since these are "ladies' wines" they may be preferred sweet, and I would suggest using 3½ lb. of sugar, but anyone preferring a medium or dry wine should reduce this quantity to 3 lb. and 2½ lb. respectively. Broom wine is certainly the better for having only 3 lb. of sugar.

Ingredients:

1 gallon { broom / cowslip / primrose / coltsfoot } flowers (heads only)
3½ lb. white sugar
2 oranges; 1 lemon
1 gallon water
Yeast; yeast nutrient

Method:

Bring the water to the boil and stir the sugar into it, making sure that it is all dissolved. Put the peel of the fruit (but no white pith) into a bowl or polythene bucket and pour the hot syrup over it, then allow the liquor to cool to 70° F. before adding the flowers, fruit juice, yeast, and yeast nutrient. (If delicate flowers are put into boiling water the wine is usually spoilt). Cover closely, and leave in a warm place for seven days, stirring each day. Then strain through a nylon sieve (or muslin) into a fermenting jar, filling it to the bottom of the neck, and fit a fermentation lock. Leave it in a warm place for three months, by which time there will be an appreciable and firm yeast deposit. Siphon the wine off the lees into a clean jar for another three months, when it can be racked again, this time into bottles if desired.

CRAB APPLE WINE (1)

Ingredients:

1 gallon crab apples
1 gallon cold water
3 lb. sugar
1 lb. raisins
1 lb. wheat
Yeast, yeast nutrient

"I call it cowslip . . ."

Method:

Wash the crab apples, then chop or crush them, and cover them with the water. Add a level teaspoon of granulated yeast and some yeast nutrient and stir it well in. Cover closely and leave in a warm place (about 70° F.), stirring well each day and mashing the apples with the hand, for 7 days.

By this time the yeast will be fully active and much increased, so stir well, then strain through a nylon sieve, or butter muslin. Enough yeast will be carried over to continue the ferment. Stir in the sugar, the chopped raisins, and the wheat, cover closely, and leave in a warm place to ferment for 14 days. Then strain into a fermentation jar and fit air-lock. Leave until the wine clears and there is a firm sediment, then siphon it off the lees into a fresh jar and refit trap. Leave for a further three months before racking again, this time into clean bottles.

CRAB APPLE WINE (2)

Ingredients:

1 gallon crab apples
3½ lb. sugar
1 gallon water
Yeast, yeast nutrient

Method:

Put the crab apples in the water and leave for three or four days (until they are well soaked) then mash them with the hand or a hardwood pulper and add the yeast and nutrient. Leave another fortnight (closely covered, of course) stirring daily, then strain the liquor on to the sugar and stir well to dissolve. If you have any kind of press it pays dividends to extract all possible juice from the pulp. Stir well to dissolve all the sugar, put into fermenting jar, and fit trap. Siphon off the lees when clear into clean bottles.

CURRANT WINE

Ingredients:

3 lb. currants
½ lb. mixed minced peel
½ lb. barley
1 gallon water
3½ lb. sugar
Yeast; nutrient

Method:

Bring the water to the boil, add the currants, peel and barley, and simmer for 15 minutes. Strain on to the sugar, and stir well to dissolve. When the liquor has cooled to 70° F. —tepid—add a vigorous yeast and yeast nutrient, pour the whole into a fermenting jar and fit trap. Keep a little aside in a cotton-wool plugged bottle for the first week or so in case the froth forces its way out through the trap; "top up" with this when the ferment quietens. Leave to ferment out, and siphon it off the lees when it clears. Refit trap and leave till wine is stable; then bottle.

CURRANT AND RAISIN WINE

Ingredients:

2 lb. currants
2 lb. raisins
1 orange; 1 lemon
1 lb. rice
3 lb. sugar
Yeast; nutrient
1 gallon water

"Just a little invention of my own"

Method:

Bring the water to the boil, add the currants, raisins. and orange peel and simmer for 20 minutes. Strain, add the rice, and simmer for four minutes. Strain on to the sugar and stir thoroughly to dissolve it, and when the liquor has cooled to 70° F., add the juice of the orange and lemon, the yeast, and some yeast nutrient. Pour into fermenting jar and fit air lock, ferment out, rack and bottle in the usual way. A variation is to use 4 lb. currants, 1 lb. raisins, 2¾ lb. sugar, and 9 pints of water: this will give a drier wine.

DAMSON WINE

Beware of recipes which you will find in some books which tell you to boil damsons, for if you overdo it you will release pectin into the wine, which will either jellify or prove almost impossible to clear, the commonest fault with plum wines. Far better just to pour the boiling water over the fruit.

Ingredients:

4 lb. damsons (or 6 lb. for really good body)
1 gallon water
3½ lb. sugar (4 lb. for sweet wine)
Yeast
Yeast nutrient

Method:

Put the water on to boil, then crush the damsons in a bowl or crock with half the sugar. Pour the boiling water over them, stir really well to dissolve the sugar, and allow to cool to about 75° F. before adding the yeast and yeast nutrient. Cover closely and leave for 48 hours in a warm place to allow the ferment to get well under way. Put the remaining sugar in a polythene bucket or other vessel and strain the liquor on to it. In this case a nylon sieve or muslin is often not fine enough and it pays to use a jelly bag, to be sure of the wine clearing.

And do not squeeze the bag to express the last of the juice, or again you will cloud the wine: give it time to run through naturally. It pays to be patient here. Stir well to make sure that all sugar is thoroughly dissolved, then pour into fermenting vessel and fit trap to allow ferment to finish. (It may be slow getting going again after you have used the jellybag, but do not worry about this: enough yeast will pass through to cause a ferment, but you must give it time to multiply again). Rack when the wine is really clear, and again three months later if a second yeast deposit is thrown. Then bottle in dark bottles. A beautiful, satisfying wine, this.

DANDELION WINE

Above all, in Spring, do not neglect to make dandelion wine, for it is an excellent accompaniment for fish and poultry, and would not disgrace anyone's table. Three trade

"Happy birthday, dear"

secrets: (1) Use the right quantity of flowers; (2) Make sure the blooms are fully open; and (3) whatever you do, do not soak them above three days, or the wine will have a foul bouquet.

Ingredients:

3 quarts flowers	**2 lemons; 1 orange**
1 gallon water	**Yeast**
3 lb. sugar	**1 lb. raisins**

Method:

Gather the flowers on a sunny day, when they are fully open (traditionally St. George's Day, 23rd April, is the time) and make your wine the same day, whilst they are fresh. Pick the heads off the stalks, leaving as little stalk as possible; there is no need to pick off individual petals, as some advocate. Put the blooms into a large bowl or crock, and pour the water, boiling, over them. Leave for three days (this is the absolute maximum, and two will do) stirring each day, and keeping the bowl closely covered. Then strain the whole into a boiler, and add the sugar and the rinds of the lemon and orange, from which you have extracted the juice. Do not include any white pith. Boil for an hour, then return to the crock, and add the juice of the lemons and orange. Allow to cool to 70° F., then add a good wine yeast, or a level teaspoon of granulated yeast, and some yeast nutrient, since this is a liquor likely to be deficient in desirable elements. Keep the crock closely covered for three days in a warm place, then strain into a fermenting jar and add the raisins before fitting a fermentation lock. Leave until the wine clears, then rack, through a sieve, into a clean jar, and leave till Christmas, by which time this wine is usually fit to drink. Another six months' storage, however (particularly in a cask), will bring a noticeable improvement.

DATE WINE

This is one of the old-fashioned recipes, but a good one, despite the variety of ingredients:

Ingredients:

1 lb. dates	**1 gallon water**
½ lb. barley	**3 lb. sugar**
1 orange	**½ nutmeg**
1 lemon	**Yeast; yeast nutrient**

Method:

Chop up the dates and slice the orange and lemon. Boil the barley in the water for ten minutes, then strain on to the dates and citrus fruit; add the half nutmeg (it should not be grated). Boil gently for 12 minutes, then strain on to the sugar, and stir well to dissolve. Cool to 70° F., add the yeast and nutrient, and keep in a warm place, closely covered, for five days, stirring daily. Then put into fermenting jar, and fit fermentation lock. Leave until it begins to clear, then rack and move into a cooler place. Rack into clean bottles when completely clear and stable.

DATE AND APRICOT WINE

Ingredients:

2 lb. dates
1 lb. dried apricots
½ lb. barley (if desired)
3 lb. sugar
1 gallon water
2 oranges; 2 lemons
Yeast; nutrient

Method:

Peel the citrus fruit and chop the dates. Bring the water to the boil, and add the fruit, citrus peel, and barley if used (barley lends body to the wine but alters the true flavour). Simmer for 10 minutes, then strain on to the sugar and juice of the oranges and lemons. Stir well, allow to cool to 70° F., then add yeast and nutrient, fit fermentation lock, and ferment right out in the usual way. Rack when it first clears, and bottle three months later. A variation is to use 3 lb. dates and omit the apricots.

ELDERBERRY-AND-BILBERRY— WITH VARIATIONS

Elderberries are excellent for making "the Englishman's port", as the wine from them is sometimes called; indeed, at one time, until the practice was made illegal, elderberries were used to improve true port. Some winemakers are occasionally disappointed in their elderberry wine because it seems unduly harsh and dry, so much so as to be almost undrinkable young, but if the wine is matured sufficiently (sometimes it needs two years) this harshness, caused by the excess tannin in this fruit, disappears. If you cannot resist drinking your elderberry wine young, the addition of a little sugar just before use effects a near-miraculous improvement!

In all the following recipes, whether for fresh or dried fruit, **bilberries** can be substituted for elderberries. They too make a glorious wine, the flavour of which many prefer to that of the elderberry.

(1) ECSTATIC ELDERBERRY

Ingredients:

4 lb. elderberries
3½ lb. white sugar
1 gallon water
Burgundy yeast; nutrient
½ oz. citric acid

Method:

To strip the berries from the stalks wear rubber gloves or use the prongs of a fork, otherwise it is a messy and tedious business. And be careful that drops of the juice do not stain your clothes because the mark seems to resist all subsequent attempts to remove it. Weigh the berries (together with any other fruit recommended in the variation recipes) and crush them in a bowl. If malt extract is being used it is added at this stage. Pour on the boiling water, stir well, and allow to cool to 70° F. before adding the yeast, acid, and nutrient. Cover closely and leave for three days in a warm place, stirring daily, then strain through a nylon sieve on to the sugar. Pour the liquor into a "grey hen" or dark glass bottle (in clear bottles the wine will lose its glorious ruby colour) but do not fill completely until the first vigorous ferment has subsided; when it has, top up with spare liquid or cold boiled water and fit fermentation lock. Leave till

"Do hurry up with the wine dear; the guests are arriving . . ."

fermentation is complete, then siphon off into clean dark bottles (if you have no dark bottles cover your white ones with a sugar bag or brown paper, or keep them in a dark cupboard) and keep for a further six months at least.

(2) ELDERBERRY ENCHANT

Ingredients:

4 lb. elderberries
3 lb. white sugar
1 lb. malt extract
½ oz. citric acid
Wine yeast culture and nutrient

Method:

As basic recipe above, except that 1 lb. malt extract is added to the "must". This gives a slightly stronger wine, with more "body".

(3) NON PAREIL
(from a French recipe)

Ingredients:

3 lb. elderberries
1 lb. damsons
3 lb. white sugar
½ oz. citric acid
Wine yeast culture and nutrient

Method:

As for Basic Recipe.

(4) "AMBROSIA"
(an eighteenth century recipe)

Ingredients:

3 lb. elderberries
1 lb. raisins
Root ginger and cloves
3 lb. sugar
½ oz. citric acid
Wine yeast culture and nutrient

Method:

Boil the root ginger and cloves in the water whilst bringing it to the boil; simmer for 15 minutes. Add the stoned raisins, then continue as indicated in basic recipe. The inclusion of the root ginger and cloves is optional and may be omitted if desired, but was greatly liked in olden days, when spicy flavours were popular.

(5) CREME DE RAISIN

Ingredients:

3 lb. elderberries
4 lb. grapes or 1 pint grape concentrate
3 lb. sugar
½ oz. citric acid
Wine yeast culture and nutrient

Method:

As for Basic Recipe.

(6) VINO MAGNIFICO

Ingredients:

3 lb. elderberries
½ bottle Semplex synthetic wine must
3 lb. sugar
½ oz. citric acid
Wine yeast culture and nutrient

Method:

As for Basic Recipe.

"I think I use rather too much of the main ingredient."

(7) ELDERBERRY AND APPLE

Ingredients:

3 lb. elderberries
4 lb. apples
3 lb. sugar
½ oz. citric acid
Yeast culture and nutrient

Method:

Wash and cut up the apples and boil 10–15 minutes in one gallon of water; then strain on to elderberries and proceed as for Basic Recipe.

(8) AS YOU LIKE IT

Ingredients:

2 lb. elderberries
2 b. blackberries
3 lb. sugar
1 oz. citric acid
Wine yeast culture and nutrient

Method:

As for Basic Recipe.

(9) AROMATIC SPLENDOUR

Ingredients:

4 lb. elderberries
1 flagon commercial cider (or more)
½ oz. citric acid
Yeast culture and nutrient
2 lb. sugar

Method:

Reduce the amount of water being used by the amount of cider added and proceed as for Basic Recipe.

(10) HERBAL NECTAR

Ingredients:

1 oz. of Heath and Heather mixed herbs
4 lb. elderberries
½ oz. citric acid
Yeast culture and nutrient

Method:

Proceed as for Basic Recipe.

ELDERBERRY (Dried) AND BANANA

(see under Banana)

(11) ELDERBERRY WINE

(from dried elderberries or bilberries)

Ingredients:

1 lb. dried elderberries (equals 4 lb. of fresh fruit)
4 lb. sugar
½ lb. raisins
1 lemon
Yeast and yeast nutrient
1 gallon water

Method:

Bring the water to the boil, and pour over the dried elderberries, 2 lb. sugar, minced raisins and lemon juice, in a crock or polythene bucket. Stir well and cover. Allow to cool to 70° F. (21° C.), then add the yeast and yeast nutrient.

"I think he found it quite a tonic"

A Bordeaux, Port, or Burgundy yeast is excellent. Fermen on the pulp for a week before straining through a nylon sieve or muslin into a fermenting jar, add remaining sugar, and make up to 1 gallon. Stir well to dissolve. Fit an air lock, and ferment in the usual way. Rack for the first time when the wine clears and again three months later.

The same recipe can be used for bilberries.

ELECAMPANE WINE
(Inula Helenium)

"The wine wherein the root of Elecampane hath steept is singular good against colicke."—Markham, *Country Farme*, A.D. 1616.

Ingredients:

1 small packet Elecampane Herb
1 marrow (2/3 lb. weight)
½ oz. citric acid (or 3 lemons, no pith, in lieu)
3½ lb. sugar
½ pint cold strong tea (or a pinch of grape tannin)
Sufficient water for 1 gallon must
Yeast nutrient and activated wine yeast

Method:

Pour boiling water over the grated or sliced marrow, including the seeds, and leave this, well covered, to soak for 24 hours. Then pour boiling water over the Elecampane herb and infuse as for tea. Strain over sugar and stir until dissolved, add the strained marrow infusion, the citric acid, cold tea, and, when cool, the yeast nutrient and activated yeast. Ferment under an air lock until it clears, then rack for the first time. Bottle when completely clear about four months later.

FENNEL WINE
(Foeniculum vulgare)

"It is much used in drink to make people more lean that are too fat."—Culpeper.

Ingredients:

1 small packet Fennel Herb
3 lb. beetroot
3½ lb. sugar
½ oz. citric acid (or 3 lemons, no pith, in lieu)
½ pint cold strong tea (or a pinch of grape tannin)
Sufficient water for 1 gallon must
Yeast nutrient and activated wine yeast

Method:

Wash the beetroot well and slice thinly, then boil in water until slightly tender, strain on to the sugar. Pour boiling water over the fennel herb and infuse as for tea. Strain on to sugared beetroot juice. When cool add the citric acid, cold tea, yeast nutrient and activated wine yeast. Ferment under an airlock until it clears, then rack for the first time. Bottle when completely clear, about 3/4 months later.

FIG WINE

Ingredients:

2 lb. dried figs
1 gallon water
3 lb. sugar
1 orange; 1 lemon
Yeast; nutrient

Method:

Soak the figs overnight in a little cold water, then make the quantity up to one gallon, bring to the boil, and simmer for five minutes. Strain, make the quantity up to 1 gallon again, and add the sugar, and the juice of the citrus fruit. When cool (70° F.) add the yeast and nutrient, and ferment under an air lock in the usual way. It will usually take about three months to clear, when it can be racked, and another two months to be ready for bottling. This is a dry wine well worth making.

FIG AND BANANA

(see under Banana)

FIG AND SULTANA (GOLDEN GLOW)

Ingredients:

2 lb. Demerara sugar
2 lb. sultanas
2 lb. figs
8 oz. barley
1 gallon water
Yeast; yeast nutrient

Method:

This makes a wine of good colour and body, and about 12% alcohol. Put the barley to soak overnight in half a pint of water. The next day mince the barley, and chop the sultanas and fruit, dropping them into a polythene bucket or crock. Meanwhile bring the gallon of water to the boil. Pour it, boiling, over the grain and fruit, and stir in the sugar. Allow to cool to 70° F. (21° C.) then add the yeast and yeast nutrient (a sherry or sauternes yeast is excellent, but failing that use a level teaspoon of granulated yeast). Ferment on the pulp for 10 days, stirring once a day, then strain through a nylon sieve or two thicknesses of muslin into a fermenting jar and fit air lock, topping up to within ¾ in. of the bottom of the cork with cold boiled water if necessary. Ferment out and rack when it clears (about eight weeks). Rack again after a further two months or so into clean bottles.

FIG AND PARSNIP

(see Parsnip and Fig)

FRUIT JUICES

(Using, see under "Concentrated Fruit Juices")

"Her Ladyship used some of her own gooseberry champagne . . ."

GINGER WINE

Ingredients:

3 oz. root ginger
2 oranges
2 lemons
$\frac{1}{2}$ lb. raisins
1 gallon water
$3\frac{1}{2}$ lb. sugar
Yeast; yeast nutrient

Method:

Peel the fruit thinly, avoiding the white pith, and put the peel and juice of the oranges and lemons into a bowl or crock, with the chopped raisins. Bring the water to the boil, and add to it the sugar and ginger, well crushed. Boil for half-an-hour, and make up once more to one gallon. Bring it to the boil again, and pour on to the rinds and fruit. Then allow the liquor to cool to 70° F. (this can be speeded by standing the crock in cold water after the first ten minutes). Add the yeast and yeast nutrient, cover and leave in a warm (65°–70° F.) place for 10 days or so. Next, strain into a fermenting jar and fit air lock. Bottle when it clears and fermentation is finished.

GINGER GLOW

Ingredients:

3 lb. sugar
$\frac{1}{2}$ oz. essence ginger
$\frac{1}{2}$ oz. essence cayenne
$\frac{1}{2}$ oz. burnt sugar or 1 pint strong tea
$\frac{1}{2}$ oz. tartaric acid
Yeast and nutrient
1 gallon water

Method:

Put the sugar in fermenting crock; add boiling water to dissolve sugar. When cool add the essences, etc., and introduce yeast and nutrient. Fit lock and ferment in usual way.

GOATS-BEARD WINE
(Tragopogon-Pratensis)
(by C. Shave)

Found in meadows, the yellow flowered goats-beard has a folk name "John go to bed at noon" due to the fact that its flowers open at 4 o'clock in the morning and close by noon. It flowers throughout June and July.

Ingredients:

1 gallon Goats-beard flowers
3½ lb. sugar
7 pints cold tea
2 lemons (or ½ oz. citric acid)
1 gallon water
Activated yeast and nutrient

Method:

Remove stalk and put the flowers in the fermentation jar with the grated lemon rinds (no pith) and sugar. Pour on the boiling water, stir to dissolve the sugar and leave to cool. Add cold tea, lemon juice or citric acid, activated yeast and yeast nutrient.

Ferment and rack in the usual way.

GOLDEN ROD WINE

"*True love lies bleeding, with the hearts-at-ease;*
And Golden Rods, and tansy running high
That o'er the pale top smiled on passer-by."

(JOHN CLARE)

Most gardens, if they have any at all, have a profusion of blooms of golden rod, and these will make an excellent wine, particularly, if it is made not too sweet: it is a glorious golden colour.

Ingredients:

- 1 pint of blossom (not pressed down)
- 3½ lb. white sugar
- ½ lb. raisins
- 1 gallon water
- 6 sweet oranges
- Yeast; yeast nutrient

Method:

Bring the water to the boil and dissolve the sugar in it, stirring for a minute or two to ensure that this is complete; then pour the boiling syrup over the flowers and raisins and add the orange juice. Allow the liquor to cool to 70° F., then add the yeast and the yeast nutrient, and leave to stand for five days, covered closely, in a temperature of about 65° F. Give it a good stir from the bottom once or twice daily. Then strain into a jar, filling it to just below the bottom of the neck, and fit a fermentation lock. When the wine has noticeably cleared, and there is an appreciable deposit, rack into a clean jar; repeat the racking three to four months later, this time into bottles. The wine will be at its best about six months later.

GRAPE AND SULTANA

Ingredients:

- 1 lb. sultanas
- 1 lb. grapes
- 3 lb. sugar
- 8 oz. barley
- 1 gallon water
- Yeast and nutrient

Method:

Soak the barley overnight in half a pint of (extra) water and the next day mince both grain and sultanas. Bring the water to the boil and pour it over the grain and fruit, then crush the grapes manually and add. Stir in the sugar and make sure that it is all dissolved. Allow to cool until just tepid (70° F. or 21° C.) then introduce the yeast, preferably a sherry yeast, and nutrient, and ferment, closely covered, for 10 days, stirring daily. Strain into fermenting jar and fit air lock and ferment out in the usual way, racking when clear, and bottling after a further two months.

GREENGAGE WINE

Plums are commonly used for wine, and it is puzzling that greengages are not more popular for the purpose, for they make a wine which many think superior in both taste and appearance to that made from "blue" plums, which often has an unattractive colour.

Ingredients:

4 lb. greengages
3½ lb. sugar
Yeast and nutrient
1 gallon water

Method:

Cut up the greengages, and pour the boiling water over them. Keep well covered for four days, mashing the fruit with the hands and stirring it well each day.

"Not when you're wearing that old lace pinny. . . . I've seen the play!"

Then strain the liquor on to the sugar, add the yeast and nutrient, and transfer to fermentation jar with trap. It is best to use a vigorously fermenting yeast starter and to start the fermentation (for three days at least) at a comparatively high temperature, between 70° F. and 75° F. Then reduce it to 65° F. Rack the wine when it clears, and repeat the process two or three months later. This is a clean, medium-sweet wine, most useful for table purposes.

HAWTHORNBERRY WINE

Ingredients:

1 gallon hawthornberries
3 lb. white sugar
Yeast and nutrient
1 gallon water
2 lemons

Method:

Wash the berries in a colander under a running tap and then place them in a bowl or crock, and bruise them with a wooden spoon or piece of hardwood. Pour over them the water (cold) and add the juice and thin peel of the lemons, being careful to exclude any white pith, which will give the wine a distinctly bitter taste.

Cover your crock closely with a folded towel and leave it for five or six days, so that the flavour can be drawn from the berries. Do not forget to give it a daily stir. Then strain on to the sugar and stir well to dissolve it. Finally add your yeast and the requisite amount of any yeast nutrient, and stir well in. Pour the yeasted liquor into a fermenting jar, filling it to the shoulder, and put the remainder by in a bottle stoppered with a plug of cotton wool. Fit fermentation trap to principal jar, and stand both in a warm place (65°–70° F.). After a week or so the ferment will have quietened and the fermenting jar can then be "topped up" as full as possible from the bottle, and the trap refitted. When the wine clears and a good yeast sediment has formed rack for the first time (this is usualy after 2½–3 months) and again, into bottles, two months later. This is distinctive and agreeable table wine.

HERBAL DELIGHT
(by C. S. Shave)

Ingredients:

1 tablespoon "Heath and Heather" mixed herbs
½ oz. citric acid
½ pint stewed tea
3½ lb. sugar
6 pints water
Yeast; yeast nutrient

Method:

Dissolve 2 lb. sugar in 6 pints of boiling water and pour over the herbs; add the citric acid, stewed tea. When cool add yeast, and yeast nutrient, and leave to ferment for 48 hours in a warm place. Strain. Then top up with sufficient strong syrup made with the remaining 1½ lb. sugar. Fit fermentation lock and ferment to completion. The wine should be racked (i.e. siphoned off the yeast deposit after about 3½ months.)

"But it's just FULL of Vitamin C."

HUCKLEBERRY WINE
(Solanum nigrum var. Guineense)

Ingredients:

3 lb. garden huckleberries	**1 gallon water**
3 lb. sugar	**Yeast and nutrient**

Method:

Pick the berries when they are fully ripe and crush them in a bowl with a wooden spoon. Add the water and mix thoroughly. Allow to stand overnight, then strain through a nylon sieve on to the sugar, and stir well to dissolve. Add yeast and nutrient, cover closely with a sheet of polythene or thick cloth, and leave in a warm place (70°–75° F.) for a week. When first vigorous ferment subsides stir, and transfer to fermenting jar. Fit fermentation lock and place in temperature of 60°–65° F. for the main fermentation. If possible use a coloured or opaque jar to keep out the light, or wrap your clear glass jar with brown paper. Rack for first time after three months, refit air lock, and rack again into clean bottles after a further three months.

KOHL RABI WINE

Ingredients:

4 lb. Kohl Rabi (early Purple Vienna variety was grown)	**3 lb. sugar**
1 orange } **or ½ oz. citric acid**	**Yeast; nutrient**
1 lemon }	

Method:

Scrub the roots well—it is not necessary to peel them—and cut them into ¼ in. slices. Put them into a large saucepan or boiler in as much of the water as possible (leaving the remainder of the gallon to one side), to bring to the boil, and simmer until tender. Do not, however, allow them to go mushy or the wine will not clear subsequently. Strain the liquor on to the remaining water, return it to the boiler, and add the sliced fruit and sugar. Simmer for half an hour, stirring well for the first few minutes, then strain through a nylon sieve or two thicknesses of muslin into a bowl or jar, and make it up to the gallon once more. Allow the liquid to cool to 70° F. (21° C.) before adding your yeast (a wine yeast, level teaspoon of granulated yeast, or ¾ oz. bakers' yeast) and nutrient, and stir well. Cover bowl closely and leave for 4 days in a warm place (about 70° F.) then put into fermenting bottle and fit air lock. After a week move into a slightly lower temperature and after three months the wine should be clearing and can be racked, or siphoned, into a clean bottle, leaving the sediment behind. Refit air lock and leave for a further three months; then rack again, this time into wine bottles, and cork securely. The same recipe can be used for turnip wine.

LAVENDER

Ingredients:

- **2 pints lavender leaves (no stalk)**
- **½ bottle Semplex concentrated wine must**
- **3–4 lb. sugar**
- **½ oz. citric acid (or 3 lemons, no pith)**
- **½ pint cold strong tea**
- **Yeast nutrient**
- **Activated yeast**
- **1 gallon water**

"Anyone seen my hydrometer?"

Method:

Pour boiling water over the lavender leaves and steep for 24 hours. Strain and warm up the liquid. Pour over the sugar and stir until the sugar is dissolved. When cool add the must, cold tea, citric acid, nutrient and yeast. Fit air lock and ferment and rack in the usual way.

LIMEFLOWER
(by C. S. Shave)

Ingredients:

Limeflower tea (Heath and Heather Pack T9)
1 lb. chopped raisins
3 lb. sugar
1 gallon water
2 lemons
2 oranges
or ½ oz. citric acid
Yeast nutrient
Yeast (selected wine)

Method:

Infuse the tea in the boiling water and leave to stand 24 hours, strain and simmer with raisins, grated orange and lemon peel (no pith). Strain on to sugar and add fruit juices or citric acid. When cool add yeast nutrient, introduce activated wine yeast and allow fermentation to proceed (using air lock) in normal way. Rack off the lees when clear.

LOGANBERRY WINE

Ingredients:

3½ lb. loganberries (or more if you have them)
3½ lb. sugar
1 gallon water
Yeast nutrient

Method:

Wash the fruit in a colander gently so as not to damage them, losing juice. Either extract the juice by means of an extractor and add the boiling water, or put them in a large bowl, pour on the gallon of water, boiling, and mash the berries with a wooden spoon. Add 1 lb. sugar, stirring well to dissolve, and allow to cool to 70° F., then introduce the yeast and yeast nutrient. Cover closely and leave for three days, stirring daily. Put the remaining 2½ lb. sugar in a bowl, and strain the fermenting juice on to it; stir well to dissolve the sugar, then pour into an opaque or dark glass fermenting jar, and fit air lock. Leave for three months, by which time it should be clearing. Rack off into a clean jar (again a dark one, to preserve the colour of the wine, which will go tawny if exposed to the light) and "top up" if necessary with boiled water or other red wine. Refit trap. Keep for another three months, then rack off again and bottle in dark bottles. A glorious, deep-red wine and the more fruit you use the more "body" it will have.

"Heavenly bouquet"

MADEIRA-TYPE WINE
(one gallon)
(by P. Duncan and B. Acton)

Ingredients:

3 lb. plums or greengages
1 pint white grape concentrate
2 lb. bananas
Madeira yeast starter, yeast nutrients
½ oz. Pectozyme
Tartaric acid and sugar syrup as required

Method:

Stone the plums, peel and chop up the bananas (discarding the skins) and mix in the grape concentrate and 1 lb. sugar. Pour about 5 pints boiling water over this mixture and when cool add the Pectozyme, yeast nutrient and actively fermenting yeast starter. Ferment on the pulp for about 3–4 days, pushing down the cap of pulp at least twice daily, then strain off the fruit, removing as much pulp debris as possible.

Check the acidity and if necessary adjust to about 4.5 parts per thousand (in terms of sulphuric acid) by means of tartaric acid (probably one-third to two-thirds of an ounce according to the ripeness of the plums).

Make a syrup of 2 lb. of sugar dissolved in 1 pint of water. Add ½ pint doses of sugar syrup whenever the gravity drops to five or below and continue feeding sugar in this way until the yeast reaches its maximum tolerance and fermentation ceases (this may take two to three months). The final volume should then be about one gallon.

After fermentation has ceased, rack the wine and place the jar in an "estufa" or hot cupboard, at 90°–130° F. for three to twelve months according to temperature, racking every three months. Finally mature the wine at normal temperatures (around 55° F.) for at least one year, racking at six-month intervals. If a dry Sercial type wine is required, the adding of sugar dosages should be stopped when the fermentation is causing a gravity drop of only one or two points per day and providing there is at least 15 per cent alcohol in the wine.

MAIZE (see Barley)

MALMSEY-TYPE WINE
(THREE gallons)
(by P. Duncan and B. Acton)

Ingredients:

1 37½p tin Grey Owl peach pulp
4 lb. beetroots
3 lb. bananas
Madeira yeast starter, yeast nutrients
1½ oz. Pectozyme
Tartaric acid and sugar syrup as required

Method:

Wash the beet and cut into hunks, peel banans and cut into slices, discarding the skins. Boil the beet and bananas in sufficient water to cover for ½ hour and strain off the boiling liquor (noting the volume) over the peach pulp plus 3 lb. sugar. Add enough cold water to make up to 2 gallons approximately. When cool add the yeast nutrients, pectozyme and actively fermenting yeast starter and ferment on the pulp for 2–3 days. Strain off the pulp, check acidity and adjust if necessary as in previous recipe and continue in the same way, topping up the volume to three gallons eventually if necessary.

"Red or white? It doesn't matter, I'm colour blind."

MINT WINE
(by C. S. Shave)

Ingredients:

- 1½ pints mint leaves (lightly bruised)
- ½ pint strong tea
- 3½ lb. sugar
- 2 lemons or citric acid
- Yeast nutrient
- Yeast
- 1 gallon water

Method:

Dissolve the sugar in the boiling water and pour this over the mint leaves, add the strong tea, lemon juice or citric acid and lemon peel (no pith). Cool to 70° F., then stir in the yeast nutrient and an activated wine yeast, or 1 level teaspoon of granulated yeast. Ferment "on the solids" for 10 days, stirring each day, then strain and place in fermentation jar with fermentation lock, and ferment in normal way.

Variations may be made by: (*a*) adding one pound chopped raisins and reducing sugar by one pound, or (*b*) adding half bottle Semplex concentrated wine must and reducing sugar by one pound.

MULBERRY WINE

Ingredients:

- 4 lb. mulberries
- 1 lb. raisins (dried figs, dates, prunes or apricots, etc., may be substituted)
- 2 oz. dried rose hips/shells (or 2 oz. dried bananas)
- 3 lb. sugar
- ½ oz. citric acid (or 3 lemons, no pith, in lieu)
- ½ pint strong tea (or a pinch of grape tannin)
- ¼ oz. pectozyme
- Water to finally make up 1 gallon of must
- Yeast nutrient and activated wine yeast

Method:

Place the berries, chopped dried fruit, rose hips and sugar into the initial fermentation vessel. Pour in the boiling water. Macerate and stir well with a wooden spoon to break up the fruits and to dissolve the sugar. When cool add the citric acid, strong tea, pectozyme and yeast nutrient. Introduce the activated wine yeast and ferment on the "pulp" for 10 days, stirring the must twice daily with a wooden spoon, and keep it closely covered. Then strain, for secondary fermentation, into fermentation vessel and fit air lock. Leave to ferment in the normal way, racking as necessary in due course.

OAKBUD WINE

Ingredients:

½ lb. oak buds and young leaves	**½ lb. raisins**
6 quarts water	**4½ lb. sugar**
½ lb. dates	**1 lemon**
	Yeast and nutrient

Method:

Gather the buds and new leaves as soon as the first leaves open. Bring the water to the boil, then add the leaves, buds, and chopped dates and raisins, and simmer for 20 minutes. Strain the liquor on to the sugar and stir well to dissolve. Allow to cool to 70° F., then add the juice of the lemon, the yeast, and the yeast nutrient. Cover closely, and ferment in a warm place for four days before transferring to fermenting jar and fitting air lock. This is an excellent wine for blending purposes, for it will add zest to an insipid wine: if it is required for this purpose reduce the sugar to 3¾ lb. to produce a dry wine.

OAK LEAF WINE

Ingredients:

1 gallon oak leaves
1 gallon boiling water
3½ lb. Sugar
2 oranges
1 lemon

Method:

Young leaves will give a different flavour from those picked later in the year when they are brown-tinted, so here, really, are two wines.

Rinse the leaves in clean cold water, then place them in a large pan or crock and pour over them the boiling water. Leave the leaves to steep for 24 hours, then strain the liquid into a boiler large enough to take both it and the sugar, with a little room to spare. Add the sugar, the juice of the fruit, and the grated peel, being careful to include no bitter white pith. Bring the whole to the boil and keep it simmering for 20 minutes. This serves the triple purpose of extracting the flavours and essences from the fruit skins, thoroughly dissolving the sugar, and sterilising the liquor. Allow to cool, strain again through a large nylon sieve or muslin, and when temperature has dropped to 70° F. add your chosen wine yeast or a level teaspoon of granulated yeast, pour into fermenting jar, and fit trap. This wine usually works vigorously, and will certainly do so if you include a little yeast nutrient as well as the fruit juice. It is therefore as well to leave little headspace in the fermenting bottle for the first four or five days, keeping a little liquor by in a cotton-wool-plugged bottle and topping up the main jar when the first vigour of the ferment has subsided; otherwise it may foam out through the trap. When the wine has cleared (usually about two to three months) siphon off the yeast sediment and keep for at least six months before use.

Walnut leaf wine can be made in the same way.

ONION WINE

Ingredients:

- ½ lb. onions
- ½ lb. potatoes
- 1 lb. chopped raisins
- 3 lb. sugar
- 2 lemons or citric acid
- Yeast nutrient
- Yeast (selected wine)
- 1 gallon water

"So much for encouraging junior to take up a hobby."

Method:

Slice and dice the onions and potatoes and place these together with the chopped raisins in warm (not hot) water in which the sugar has been dissolved. Add lemon juice (no pith) or citric acid and yeast nutrient, then introduce activated yeast. Ferment for 10 days, then strain and complete fermentation in glass jars under fermentation lock.

ORANGE AND WHEAT

Ingredients:

6 Jaffa oranges
1 lb. wheat
¼ lb. raisins
1 lemon
1 gallon water
3 lb. sugar
Yeast; nutrient

Method:

Bring the water to the boil, then simmer the skins of the citrus fruit in it for a quarter of an hour. Take out the peel and pour the liquid over the sugar, the juice of the oranges and lemon, the washed wheat, and the chopped raisins. Allow to cool to 70° F. (21° C.) before adding the yeast and yeast nutrient, and keep well covered in a warm place, stirring daily, for 10 days. Then strain into fermenting jar, fit trap, and ferment out, rack and bottle in the usual way.

SEVILLE ORANGE WINE

Ingredients:

6 Seville oranges
6 sweet oranges
3½ lb. white sugar (3 lb. for a dry wine)
1 gallon water
Yeast; nutrient

Method:

Wash the oranges and peel three of each, keeping the peel thin and avoiding the pith, which imparts a very bitter flavour. Boil a quart of water and then add the peel to it;

cover, and allow to stand for 24 hours to extract the zest. Then strain the infusion into a crock or polythene bucket containing the remainder of the gallon of water, the sugar, and the juice of all twelve oranges. Stir until all the sugar is dissolved, and then add the yeast and yeast nutrient. Cover the bowl closely and stand in a warm place (70° F. or 21° C.) for four or five days, after which the ferment will have quietened a little and the liquor can be poured into a fermenting jar and a trap fitted. Leave until it clears, then rack and bottle as usual.

SWEET ORANGE WINE

Ingredients:

12 sweet oranges	**1 lb. large raisins**
1 lemon	**1 gallon water**
4 lb. sugar	**Yeast; nutrient**

Method:

Peel half the oranges and put the skins in the oven, baking them until they are browned; then pour over them a quart of the water, boiling. Peel the remaining oranges, and then pulp all the oranges in a crock or polythene bucket. Add the chopped or minced raisins and the Campden tablet, and pour over the fruit the remainder of the water, cold, and the liquid from the orange-peel infusion. Stir well, cover closely, and leave for 24 hours. Add the lemon juice, yeast, nutrient, and 1 lb. sugar, stirring well to dissolve. Stir the must daily and keep in a warm place (70° F., 21° C.). After four days strain on to remaining sugar, stirring well to dissolve, and pour into fermenting jar. Fit trap, and ferment at roughly 65° F. (18° C.) until clear; then rack. Keep a further two months under air lock before bottling.

PARSLEY AND RICE
(by Humfrey Wakefield)

Ingredients:

½ lb. raisins
1 quart measure parsley (packed tight)
¼ lb. rice
2–2½ lb. sugar
Grated rind of 2 oranges
Grated rind and juice of 1 lemon
Nutrient salt (as instructed)
Tokay yeast
Amylozyme, or Pectasin, as instructed

Method:

Boil parsley (well washed) in ½ gallon water. Put in rice and simmer further five minutes. Strain through coarse sieve on to sugar, grated rinds, lemon juice and coarsely chopped raisins. Stir well. When cool, add yeast (previously propagated in a starter bottle), and Pectasin (or Amylozyme) dissolved in a little warm water.

Add water if necessary to bring bulk of must up to near a gallon.

Ferment on raisin-pulp for 2–4 days, stirring frequently, and keeping covered.

Strain off into gallon jar through coarse sieve, and top up (if necessary) with water. Fit lock. Rack when wine begins to clear, and again when fermentation is quite finished.

Produces a light, fragrant white table wine, something between pineapple and apricot. Don't worry about chicken-broth smell in early stages. It ferments out. If sweet dessert wine is wanted (also good), add a further 1 to 1½ lb. sugar when fermentation begins to slow.

PARSNIP WINE

Ingredients:

7 lb. parsnips	**2½ gallons water**
3 lb. sugar to each gallon of liquor	**Yeast and nutrient**
	2 lemons

Method:

Scrub the parsnips and scrape them quickly with a strong knife, then slice them and boil them in the water (or some of it) until just tender, but on no account so long that they go mushy, or the wine will not clear. If the roots are boiled in half the water, for convenience sake, the remainder can be added later.

Strain through a large nylon sieve, or muslin tied over a pan, on to the remaining water (cold) but do not press the parsnips or hurry the process unduly, or again the wine may not clear. Measure your resulting liquor, and add 3 lb. white sugar to each gallon, and the juice of two lemons. Bring to the boil and then turn down the heat and simmer gently for three-quarters of an hour. Turn into a crock or pan, and allow to cool to 70° F.; then add yeast and yeast nutrient, preferably a wine yeast, but a level teaspoon of granulated yeast can be employed failing anything better. Cover closely with a thick cloth, and keep in a warm place for a week (60°–70° F.). Then pour into fermenting jar and fit air lock. Rack when it clears, and refit air lock, and rack for the second time after a further three months.

PARSNIP WINE (Spiced)

Ingredients:

- **7 lb. parsnips**
- **3 lb. sugar**
- **1 lemon**
- **2 oranges**
- **1 gallon water**
- **1 oz. root ginger**
- **Yeast; yeast nutrient**

Method:

Midwinter is the time to make this wine, for the sugar content of the roots will have been concentrated by the winter frosts. Scrape or scrub the parsnips clean (a strong-bladed, large knife is a great help), slice them, and boil until tender, but not mushy. (Be careful not to overdo the boiling or you will subsequently have difficulty clearing the wine. If you have a press you need boil for only 5–10 minutes, for you can then press the parsnips afterwards). The bruised ginger and the thinly-pared rinds of the citrus fruit are boiled in with the parsnips (or separately, in a quart or so of the water if you are using the press; this is then added to the remainder). Strain all the liquid on to the juice of the fruit and dissolve the sugar in it, stirring well. Cool to 70° F. (or 21° C.) then add the yeast and yeast nutrient, and cover. Stir daily. Four or five days later, stir, and pour into fermenting jar, and fit trap. Leave in a warm place to ferment until the wine clears and a yeast deposit has formed (about two months) and then rack for the first time. Refit trap and leave until completely clear and stable (another two months or so) then rack again and bottle.

PARSNIP AND BANANA
(see under Banana)

PARSNIP AND FIG

Ingredients:

4 lb. parsnips
1 lb. dried figs
½ lb. raisins
½lb. rice
3 lb. sugar
1 gallon water
Yeast and yeast nutrient

Method:

Scrub or scrape the parsnips, slice them, and boil them in the water with the chopped figs and raisins until only just tender, usually not more than 20 minutes. Do not "over-cook" so that the parsnips go soft and mushy, or the wine may subsequently be difficult to clear. Then strain the liquor on to the rice, bring to the boil, and boil for four minutes. Strain on to the sugar and stir well to dissolve. Allow the liquor to cool to 70° F. then add the yeast—a sherry yeast

"We HATE small glasses."

is excellent—and yeast nutrient, and pour into a fermenting jar or bottle. Fill to shoulder, fitting an air lock, and keep the remainder of the liquor on one side, also under a fermentation lock. After about a week in a temperature of 65°–70° F. the first vigorous ferment will have subsided and the jar can be topped up with the spare liquor, now being filled to the bottom of the neck, and the trap re-inserted. When the wine begins to clear and a yeast deposit has formed (6 weeks to 2 months) siphon it off the less into a fresh bottle and refit lock. Leave for a further three months before bottling. This will usually produce a dry wine if a good nutrient has been used, and some readers may care to add 4–8 ozs. more sugar either before fermentation ceases or to the finished wine.

PARSNIP AND BEETROOT

(see under Beetroot and Parsnip)

PEACH PERFECTION

This is a recipe by Mrs. Cherry Leeds, of Thames Ditton, for a peach wine which is so superb—and *cheap*—that we give the fullest possible instructions . . .

It sounds extravagant, but it is not. Keep an eye on the greengrocer's and you'll see that in August (usually about the first fortnight) peaches come right down in price, to 5p each or even less. The wine works out at about 7p a bottle.

Mrs. Leeds uses a Kitzinger sherry or Tokay yeast, and here we give again her recipes, for the benefit of the many readers who have requested them:

TO MAKE 10 GALLONS

Ingredients:

30 lb. peaches	**3 oz. citric acid**
32 lb. sugar (10 Demerara)	**1½ teaspoons tannin**
Boiling and boiled water	**3 oz. Pectozyme**

Method:

Wipe peaches and remove the stones; drop into large container such as a polythene bin. Scrub hands well and squeeze the peaches until well mashed. Well cover with boiling water and leave covered overnight.

The next day stir in the Pectozyme and cover well. On the third day strain through muslin, twice if possible to reduce sludge, and put into the 10-gallon jar; add citric acid, tanning and nutrient.

At this point it is a simple matter to place the jar or carboy into the position it will occupy during fermentation. Put 20 lb. of sugar into the large container and add sufficient boiling water to dissolve, and when cool add to the jar. Then the level of the liquid is brought up to the turn of the shoulder

"Grape? Haven't you got any PROPER wine?"

of the jar with boiled water. Open the yeast bottle, pour in, and fit fermentation lock. The gravity at this stage will be about 100; the original gravity is almost invariably 25–30. Fermentation will start on the third day if the temperature is sufficient (70°–75° F.).

The rest of the sugar is added in stages from now on, the first addition of four pints of syrup when the gravity is 30, that is, roughly, after two weeks. The sugar is then added in two-pint lots when the gravity is between 10 and 15 each time. The syrup used is 2 lb. sugar to one pint boiling water and cooled, thus making two pints syrup.

The fermenting period lasts for about seven or eight months, though one can keep it going for a year with small additions of syrup.

"Emergency Ward 10? No, just the Winemakers' Circle committee meeting"

The first racking takes place when all the sugar is in and the reading is 10. Some of the wine will have to be removed to accommodate the last two pints of syrup. Stir up the jar and remove half a gallon. Put it by, under an air lock, and this can be used to top up the jar after the first racking. Stir the liquid vigorously with an oak rod once a day for the first few weeks.

Because of the Pectozyme used the wine will clear perfectly and after the first racking will become crystal clear, but don't be tempted to rack again until fermentation has ceased finally. This usually happens when the gravity is about five.

The alcoholic content will be about 18%.

"Just a shade too effervescent"

TO MAKE FIVE GALLONS

For the 5-gallon jars use half quantities except the Pectozyme—this is 2 ounces—otherwise the procedure is the same.

TO MAKE ONE GALLON

Ingredients:

3 lb. peaches
1 teaspoon citric acid
½ oz. Pectozyme
Saltspoon tannin
3 lb. sugar
½ gallon boiling water

Method:

The method is the same but the yeast starter bottle is prepared on the same day as mashing, and the sugar is put in all together, just before the yeast starter.

PINEAPPLE AND BEET

(see under Beet and Pineapple)

PLUM WINE (1)

Ingredients:

4 lb. plums
3½ lb. white sugar
1 gallon water
Yeast

Method:

Wash the fruit and cut it up, then put it in a bowl and pour over it the water, boiling. Cover it with a thick cloth or sheet of polythene, and leave four days, giving it an occasional stir. Then strain through a nylon sieve or muslin, dissolve the sugar in the juice, and add yeast. Cover again, and two days later pour into fermenting jar and fit trap. When the wine clears siphon it off the lees, keep for a further three months, then rack into bottles. More fruit (say 6 lb. to the gallon) can be used if available to lend more body to the wine, or, failing that, a pound of wheat or barley (plum wine does tend to be rather thin).

PLUM WINE (2)

Ingredients:

4 lb. plums	4 cloves
1 lemon	¼ oz. root ginger
3 lb. sugar	1 gallon water
	Yeast and nutrient

Method:

This is basically a very old recipe, from the days when additional flavourings were favoured, and to our mind the cloves and ginger are just as well omitted, but we give the entire recipe, as listed.

Cut up the plums, removing the stones, and add to them the crushed ginger, the cloves, and the sliced lemon. Bring the water to the boil and pour it over these ingredients,

and stir. Cover and leave for three or four days, stirring twice daily. Strain through double muslin on to the sugar, stir to dissolve it, and add the yeast and nutrient. Put into fermenting jar, fit trap, and leave to ferment to a finish in a warm place. When clear and stable siphon off into clean bottles and cork.

CHERRY PLUM WINE

by Mrs. Dorothy Cuthbertson (Liverpool Guild)

The Liverpool Guild were so impressed by this cheap-to-make wine (cherry plums sell for as little as 6d. a lb. in season) that they suggested Mrs. Cuthbertson have the recipe published. It makes, she says, a wine very similar to a Sauternes. Here it is:

Ingredients:

5 lb. cherry plums, 1 lb. raisins (chopped)
2 teaspoons citric acid
2–3 lb. sugar (according to taste)
¼ teacup of strong tea
Respora all-purpose yeast
Leigh-Williams yeast food

"Some of these old recipes use large quantities . . ."

Method:

Wash fruit, cover with one gallon boiling water, add 2 lb. sugar, tea, raisins, citric acid; when cool add yeast starter and yeast food. Stir and squeeze the fruit daily for five days, then strain into fermentation jar and fit lock. Add sugar in syrup form as required. (Not more than 1 lb. dissolved in half pint of water.)

Keep the fermentation going as long as possible, but when it finally ceases and the wine is clear and stable siphon into clean bottles.

PORT-TYPE WINE
(by P. Duncan and B. Acton)

Ingredients:

3 lb. elderberries
2 lb. bananas
1 pint red grape concentrate
Tartaric acid, nutrient, sugar syrup as required
Port yeast

Method:

Mash elderberries to extract juice, and leach pulp with 1 pint cold water. Boil bananas in 2 pints water and add liquor to elderberry juice plus leachings and grape concentrate. Bring volume up to 7 pints and adjust acid to between 3.5 and 4.0 parts per thousands as sulphuric acid (this requires the addition of ½ oz. tartaric acid). Add yeast nutrient when cool and a good port yeast culture, and feed with additions of syrup in quarter-pint lots (syrup made with 2 lb. sugar in 1 pint of water) whenever the wine tastes dry (or drops in gravity to 5). When fermentation is almost finished, rack and top up to 1 gallon with water and syrup so that the final gravity is around 10. This, for those who do not use a hydrometer, would mean adding a final quarter-pint of syrup, or a little more.

In view of the relatively high cost of this wine, it will be worth keeping for at least two years, and preferably three, racking at three-month intervals in order that the maximum flavour and smoothness may develop.

An equally satisfactory Port-type wine can be made by using 3 lb. blackberries, 2 lb. sloes or damsons, and 1 lb. elderberries, mashing and leaching these and then proceeding as above.

For a tawny wine, use 6 lb. blackberries only and keep finished wine for three or four years.

PRIMROSE

(see Cowslip)

PRUNE WINE

(by H. E. Bravery)

Ingredients:

6 lb. prunes
2 lemons
3½ lb. sugar
9 pints water
1 oz. yeast

Method:

Wash the prunes in water and put them in the fermenting vessel. Boil 2 lb. of sugar in 7 pints of water and pour over the fruit while boiling. Allow to cool and add the yeast. Cover and ferment for 10 days, crushing well each day as soon as the fruit has become soft.

After 10 days, crush well and strain out the solids. Wring out as dry as you can and put the strained liquor into a gallon jar.

Boil the rest of the sugar in the remaining two pints of water and when cool add to the rest. Cover or fit fermentation lock and leave until all fermentation has ceased.

PRUNE AND BANANA

(see under Banana)

PRUNE AND WHEAT WINE

(by Syd Lowe)

Ingredients:

- 1 lb. prunes (best quality)
- 1 lb. wheat (best quality)
- ¼ lb. raisins
- 3 lb. sugar
- 1 yeast nutrient tablet
- 1 gallon water
- 2 Vitamin B tablets (Aneurine hydrochloride B.P.)
- Yeast, sherry yeast (or 1 level teaspoon dried yeast)

Method:

Cut each prune through with a knife into a bucket or crock. Place wheat in a moderate oven to lightly bake (do not allow to brown over), then add to prunes, with yeast nutrient, raisins and Vitamin B. Pour on 1 gallon of water that has been boiled and allowed to cool, cover, and stir very thoroughly every day for 10 days. Strain and press pulp to extract all the juice. (Do this with your hands if no other means available). Add 2 lb. sugar (if made into syrup with small amount of warm water it is easier to blend in). Add yeast, stir thoroughly to mix.

Leave this in a warm place for about 10 days, then strain through muslin or jelly bag into gallon jar and fit air lock. After it has been in the jar for about 10 days, sample it and, if necessary, add a little of the 1 lb. of sugar from the main recipe that you have left. Repeat this after another 10 days; then add the balance of the 3 lb. sugar.

Leave until fermentation is complete. Strain into clean jar, fit cork, and leave in cool place (a cellar is ideal) until it clears perfectly; then bottle.

PUMPKIN WINE

Ingredients:

- 5 lb. pumpkin
- 3 lb. white sugar
- 2 lemons
- 2 oranges
- Yeast
- 1 gallon water
- 1 oz. root ginger (this can be omitted if desired)

Method:

Grate the pumpkin, slice the oranges and lemons, bruise the ginger and put them all into a jug or crock. Pour over the boiling water and when cool add the yeast. Allow to stand for five days closely covered, stirring frequently, then strain and dissolve the sugar in the liquid. Either put it into a fermentation jar and fit trap, or keep it closely covered and then ferment in the usual way. When it clears siphon off the yeast. The pumpkin wine should be ready after about six months and then can be bottled.

RED CURRANT WINE (1)

This is a popular wine and well worth making, but often tends to turn out disappointingly "thin" for those who prefer good body in their wines. If you require a delicate wine, make it according to the recipe, but if you want a slightly heavier

"... but I only drink a gallon of it a day ..."

wine, use an additional pound of fruit, half a pound of rolled barley (most mills can supply it) and pour the water on boiling instead of cold.

Ingredients:

3 lb. red currants	**1 gallon water**
4 lb. white sugar	**Yeast**

Method:

Put the fruit in a bowl and crush thoroughly, then add the cold water and 1 crushed Campden tablet. (Omit the tablet if using the grain and boiling water.) Leave standing, covered, of course, for six or seven days, stirring daily. Then strain through a nylon sieve or jellybag, expressing as much juice as possible, into the fermenting vessel. Add the sugar, stirring well to dissolve it, yeast and nutrient, fit a fermentation lock, and leave in a temperature of about 70° F. to ferment. Rack the wine off the lees when it clears, refit the air lock, and repeat the process about three months later, when it will probably be stable and ready to bottle. Again, dark bottles will preserve its delicate colour.

RED CURRANT WINE (2)

Ingredients:

4 lb. red currants	**3½ lb. sugar**
7 pints water	**Yeast and nutrient**

Method:

As for cherry or blackcurrant.

RHUBARB (1)
GOLDEN PIPKIN
(by C. Shave)

Ingredients:

3 lb. red rhubarb	**2 lemons or 1 teaspoon citric acid**
½ pint strong tea	
3 lb. sugar	**Yeast nutrient**
½ bottle Semplex concentrated wine must	**Yeast (selected wine)**

Method:

Using rhubarb picked mid-May prepare as for "Golden Dream" (see p. 99), adding the concentrated wine must, yeast nutrient and some strongly working selected wine yeast fermenting in the normal way. This is another tried and tested favourite—one of those wines of which one never seems to have enough. It is always a case of "All gone already?" or "Not quite mature yet!"

RHUBARB (2)
MEMORABLE NECTAR

Ingredients:

- 6 lb. red rhubarb, picked mid-May
- 1 lb. raisins
- ½ pint strong tea
- Yeast nutrient and yeast (selected wine)
- 4 lb. sugar
- 2 lemons or 1 teaspoon citric acid

Method:

Prepare rhubarb juice as in "Golden Dream". The raisins should be cut up and simmered in the strong tea and the pulp strained into the rhubarb juice. As raisins are being used in this recipe extract of malt should not be added. After dissolving the sugar and adding the lemon juice and/or citric acid to the juice add the yeast nutrient and a working wine yeast; ferment in the normal way.

Very popular in the Midlands and another of my favourites.

Rhubarb wine contains an excess of unpleasant oxalic acid, and this is best removed before fermentation by stirring in 1 oz. per gallon of precipitated chalk, or powdered cuttlefish. The juice will effervesce. If afterwards it still has an acid taste add up to another ½ oz., but not more. Finally, to give you the acidity you need, add the juice of three lemons, or one heaped teaspoon of citric acid. A little more may be necessary; taste the juice, and remember that a quarter of the acidity present will be lost during fermentation; allow for this, and adjust the acidity so that it is that much too pronounced. Then add the sugar.

RHUBARD (3)
"GOLDEN DREAM"

Ingredients:

6 lb. red rhubarb
1 lb. malt extract
4 lb white sugar
½ pint strong tea
2 lemons (or citric acid)
Yeast nutrient
Yeast (selected wine)

Method:

Whether or not the oxalic acid is removed by precipitated chalk is a matter of opinion, I have made it with or without! The rhubarb stalks should be picked in mid-May and as malt extract is being used raisins should not be added to this recipe.

Do not peel the rhubarb but wipe the stalks clean, cut into small short lengths and cover with cold or warm (not boiling) water and soak for three days, crushing the rhubarb with the hands after the second day. Then strain off into fermenting vessel. Dissolve sugar and malt extract, adding this with tea and lemons, or one teaspoon of citric acid to the strained rhubarb juice. Add yeast nutrient and an activated wine yeast and ferment in the normal way.

An often repeated recipe for a favourite "golden" wine with "body".

"CHRISTMAS PORT"

Having made in May either "Golden Dream" or "Memorable Nectar" and given it its first racking it will be blackberry time.

Pick 3 lb. blackberries and cover them with one pint boiling water, adding ¼ lb. sugar, then squeeze pulp through muslin and add the juice to the racked rhubarb wine. Fit fermentation lock and ferment on in the usual way.

A most satisfying wine.

"WINTER CHEER"

Ingredients:

6 lb. red rhubarb (picked mid-May)
1 quart balm leaves or 1 packet dried leaves (Heath and Heather)
4 lb. sugar
2 lemons or 1 teaspoon citric acid
Yeast nutrient
Yeast (selected wine)
½ pint strong tea

Method:

Prepare rhubarb juice as in "Golden Dream". Put balm leaves in saucepan with water and bring to boil with lemon peel (no pith), cutting off heat as soon as water is boiling allow to stand for 15 minutes, strain and add this to rhubarb juice, pouring over dissolved sugar, lemon juice or citric acid and strong tea. Add yeast nutrient and a selected wine yeast started fermenting in normal way.

"Winter Cheer" may be varied by the addition of 1 lb. of malt extract to the gallon, giving more body, or 1 lb. of raisins for eventually that grand old-time mellow flavour.

RICE WINE

(Wheat, or rye, can be substituted if desired)

Ingredients:

To make two gallons:

8 oz. rice (wheat, rye)
7 lb. sugar
2 gallons water
1/3rd oz. citric acid
1 pkt. Vierka sherry yeast
1 pkt. Vierka nutrient salt
1 Campden tablet

Method:

Two or three days in advance prepare a starter for the yeast by bringing one pint apple juice to the boil with a pinch of nutrient salt and a tablespoon of sugar. Add yeast and leave, plugged with cotton wool, in a temperature of 70° F.

On the third day after starting the yeast, boil 8 oz. rice in five pints water with the addition of two tablespoonfuls sugar, for five minutes only. Allow to cool, and add the yeast starter, now in full ferment, together with the one teaspoon nutrient salt, and 1/3 oz. citric acid (about three level teaspoonsful).

By the next day the rice-pulp is in vigorous fermentation. Add what remains of the sugar (7 lb. less three tablespoons) dissolved in the rest of the water (two gallons less five pints), and pour into a clean fermenting jar. Strain the fermenting pulp on to the syrup (when cool), through a clean linen bag or handkerchief, with the help of a funnel. Press out lightly with the hands, so that some of the rice-starch goes into the jar.

"I don't think it really matters HOW you serve wine, do you?"

Don't fill to the brim yet, but leave room for foaming. If need be keep back some of the syrup till the tumultuous ferment has died down, say after 14 days.

The wine will take about two months to ferment right out. Then is the time for the first racking. Top up with pure water, and allow a further four weeks in the warm for the secondary fermentation. Rack again, lightly sulphite with the Campden tablet, and put in the cool for another four weeks.

The wine will then be as clear as water, and can be coloured lightly with edible colouring matter, or blackcurrant iuice, before drawing off into bottles.

RICE WINE (Chinese)

Ingredients:

3 lb. paddy rice (polished rice will not do)
3 lb. honey
1 gallon water
The juice of 2 lemons, 2 oranges
(These quantities are the suggested ones; precise amounts were not given in the original Chinese recipe.)

Method:

"Steep the grain for 20 days in water, stirring every day, and keeping well covered. Bring it to the boil and boil it gently until the grains are soft and pulpy, then put it into an earthenware crock (with your gallon of water). To the must are then added various fruits and flowers, and a percentage of honey to give strength, aroma and colour to the wine.

"In China whence comes this recipe, lemon or lime flower are added according to the taste of the maker, the juice of oranges or lemons, and the thinly peeled rinds.

"When the must is all well blended and has cooled yeast is added and it is allowed to ferment in a jar for several days. The wine is then strained into clean, glazed vessels, where by a second ferment it clears itself. When the ferment in the second jar is finished, the wine is drawn off into small earthenware jars which are sealed down and set aside to mature. Well made, this wine is very strong in alcohol content and will keep for many years. It can be distilled (but not in this country!) into the Chinese spirit called Sam Choo."

RICE WINE
(English version!)

Steep 3 lb. of wholemeat, or paddy rice, in half a gallon of water for six days, stirring every day. Then put into another bowl 3 lb. of sugar, the juice and rind of two or three lemons and oranges, and, if liked, a few spice. Pour a gallon of boiling water on to the fruit and sugar and stir until it is all blended; then strain the water from the rice and add it to the mixture. When the liquor has cooled to about 70° F. add yeast, cover the bowl and leave for 24 hours. Then strain carefully into a cask and leave in a warm place to finish the ferment. Top up each morning with water and drop in a stoned raisin each day when the fermentation begins to flag. When all movement has ceased, bung down the cask and store for a year.

RICE AND BANANA

(see under Banana)

RICE AND PARSLEY

(see Parsley and Rice)

RICE

(see Barley)

ROSEHIP WINE

Ingredients:

3½ lb. rosehips	**1 gallon boiling water**
3 lb. white sugar	**Yeast; yeast nutrient**

Method:

Wash your rosehips thoroughly in a colander, and then either cut them in half or crush them with a piece of wood. A good way of tackling this rather tricky job is to use a domestic mincer with the outer cutting disc removed. Use the fixed disc with the largest holes and this will just neatly crush the pips. To do so by hand with a mallet or roller is rather a sticky and messy business! Put the crushed rosehips and sugar into a crock or polythene dustbin and pour over them the boiling water; stir well until the sugar is completely dissolved.

Allow the liquor to cool to about 70° F. (cool enough for you to be able to put your finger in it comfortably) and add your yeast, an all-purpose wine yeast or, failing that, a level teaspoon of granulated yeast, together with some yeast nutrient. Cover the container closely with a thick cloth or polythene and leave in a warm place for a fortnight, stirring daily.

Then strain through a nylon sieve or two thicknesses of butter muslin into a fermentation jar, and fit an air lock. This wine usually ferments very vigorously, and will normally clear after about three months. Siphon it into a fresh jar, not disturbing the sediment, and leave for a further three months before bottling.

ROSEHIP (Dried)

Ingredients:

13 oz. dried rosehips
2½ lb. sugar
Juice of 1 lemon
Tokaier yeast and yeast nutrient
1 gallon water

Method:

Dried rosehips can now be purchased in this country and one can thus avoid the tedious business of picking fresh hips. The dried ones make a wine fully as good, and rosehip wine *is* good, indeed the Germans hold that it is second only to the grape for winemaking. With the dried rosehips, which have been largely dehydrated, and therefore weigh less, a smaller quantity is required than when one uses the fresh fruit.

Prepare your yeast starter two days before making the wine and soak the rosehips overnight in 1 pint of water.

"... and now a few words about mead ..."

Mince your rosehips through an ordinary domestic mincer with the outer cutting disc removed and put into a bowl with the sugar and lemon juice. Pour over them the water, boiling. Stir well to dissolve the sugar. When the mixture has cooled to 70° F., add your fermenting Tokaier yeast. Cover closely with a polythene sheet secured by elastic and stand in a warm place (about 70° F.) but stir daily. After 10 days, strain into a one-gallon jar, topping up with cold boiled water to the bottom of the neck if necessary, and fit fermentation lock. When the wine clears rack into a clean jar and refit lock. Leave for a further three months, then rack into clean bottles and cork down.

ROSEHIP SHELL AND FIG

Ingredients:

6–8 oz. dried rosehip shells
4 oz. dried figs
3½ lb. sugar
(2 lb. for a dry wine)
Tokaier yeast

Method:

Put the figs in just enough water to cover them and leave overnight. The next day add a little more water, bring to the boil, and simmer for 10 minutes. Strain the juice into a saucepan and make quantity up to 1 gallon. Bring to the boil and pour over the rosehip shells, sugar and lemon juice. Stir well to dissolve sugar. Allow to cool to 70° F. and then add your yeast. Cover closely with a polythene sheet secured by elastic and stand in a warm place (about 70° F.) for 10 days, stirring daily. Then strain into fermenting jar and fit air lock. Ferment until the wine clears and fermentation slows, then rack into a clean jar, and refit lock. Rack again after three months into clean bottles, and cork down.

ROSEHIP AND DRIED BANANA

(see under Banana)

ROSEHIP SHELL AND BANANA

(see under Banana)

ROSEHIP SYRUP

Ingredients:

1 small bottle rosehip syrup	2½ lb. sugar
7 pints water	Yeast and nutrient

Method:

Rosehip syrup provides an easy way of making wine, and a 6 oz. or 8 oz. bottle is sufficient to make a gallon. Brands commonly available are Delrosa (in 6 oz. and 12 oz. bottles), Hipsy (in 8 oz.) and Optrose (8 oz. and 14 oz.). Merely bring the water to the boil, add the syrup and sugar, and stir well to dissolve. Cool to 70° F., and add the yeast and nutrient. Pour into fermenting jar and fit air lock. Leave in a warm place. After a week top up to bottom of neck with cold boiled water and refit lock. Ferment, rack, and bottle in usual way.

"There MUST be an easier way."

ROSEMARY WINE
(Rosmarinus officinalis)

"There's rosemary, that's for remembrance.' SHAKESPEARE

Ingredients:

1 small packet Rosemary Herb
½ oz. citric acid (or 3 lemons, no pith, in lieu)
3½ lb. sugar
½ pint cold strong tea (or a pinch of grape tannin)
¼ bottle Semplex synthetic must
Sufficient water for 1 gallon must
Yeast nutrient and activated wine yeast

Method:

Pour boiling water over the Rosemary Herb and infuse as for tea. Strain on to sugar and stir to dissolve sugar. When cool add the strong tea, citric acid and synthetic must. Then when cool add the yeast nutrient and activated wine yeast. Fit air lock to fermenting vessel and leave until it clears. Rack and bottle in due course, 3/4 months later.

"... he's a keen winemaker."

SARSAPARILLA AND BANANA

(see under Banana)

SAUTERNES

(by P. Duncan and B. Acton)

Ingredients:

2 lb. bananas
3 lb. ripe gooseberries or apricots (or 37½p tin of Grey Owl Apricot Pulp)
1 pint white grape concentrate
¾ pint elderflowers or a packet of dried flowers
1½ fl. oz. glycerol (obtained at any chemist as glycerine)
Yeast nutrient
1/10th oz. tannin
Sauternes yeast
Sugar syrup as required, made by boiling 2 lb. sugar with 1 pint water
Acid as required to produce acidity 5.2 p.p.t. sulphur; or if not using acid testing kit, between ¼ oz. and ¾ oz. acid (equal parts malic acid and tartaric acid or a citric/malic/tartaric mixture). Riper fruit will require the addition of more acid than less ripe fruit.
Water to 1 gallon.

"Have you been at my runner bean again?"

Method:

Peel bananas and boil (with skins) in two pints of water for half an hour. Put concentrate, fruit and flowers in a plastic bucket and strain boiling liquor from bananas over them. When cool bring liquid content up to about six pints. Add ¼ oz. citric acid, tannin, glycerol and nutrient and then add a vigorously fermenting Sauternes yeast starter. After three days strain off fruit and continue fermentation in a fermenting jar or other container closed with an air lock adding ¼ pint doses of sugar syrup whenever wine goes dry (or gravity drops to below 10). If fermentation proceeds longer than eight weeks, make a preliminary racking with plenty of splashing to aerate the wine and add further nutrients to continue fermentation to its final point. When fermentation ceases, rack and sulphite 100 parts per million (two Campden tablets per gallon). Mature for at least a year, preferably in cask, racking at three-monthly intervals and sulphiting each time (50 p.p., or 1 Campden tablet).

SHERRY
(Dry Fino type)
(by P. Duncan and B. Acton)

Ingredients:

1 lb. bananas
1 pint white grape concentrate
½ oz. tartaric acid
1 oz. gypsum (calcium sulphate)
Yeast nutrient
Sugar to be added as below
2 lb. parsnips, turnips or carrots
½ oz. cream of tartar
Good sherry yeast culture
½ oz. Pectozyme
1 gallon water

Method:

Peel bananas and chop root vegetables and boil both in three pints of water for half an hour. Strain liquor over grape concentrate, tartaric acid and cream of tartar (stir until latter dissolves). When cool add gypsum and yeast nutrient with vigorous stirring, and adjust gravity of must with syrup and water until you have one gallon at a gravity of between 110 and 120. Add yeast and Pectozyme and endeavour to obtain a long cool fermentation lasting up to two months.

Rack carefully into a container large enough to ensure a good air space above the wine and plug container with cotton wool. Keep in a temperature of 55° F. to 65° F. undisturbed by any movement for at least one year. If a flor forms, tasting must be done by carefully cutting a small hole in the yeast skin.

SHERRY
(Oloroso type)
(by P. Duncan and B. Acton)

Ingredients:

2 lb. bananas	**1 lb. chopped raisins**
3 lb. peaches	**½ oz. tartaric acid**
Yeast nutrient	**Sherry wine yeast culture**

Sugar syrup to be added as below (syrup made by boiling up 2 lb. sugar with 1 pint water)

Method:

Peel bananas and boil in four pints of water for half an hour. Strain water while boiling over raisins and peaches.

Mix in tartaric acid and leave to cool for 12 hours. Add nutrient and a vigorously fermenting yeast starter. Ferment on pulp for three days then strain off pulp into gallon jar, pressing fruit lightly, and bring volume up to seven pints. Check gravity periodically and add quarter pint doses of sugar syrup every time the gravity falls to 5.

When fermentation is complete, rack very carefully and place in container larger than amount of wine, allowing good air space and plug with cotton wool plug only. Leave in a warm place (around 75° F.) for at least three months (or longer if temperature is cooler than this). A flor should not normally develop in this case but a good sherry flavour will result.

Sweeten to taste when bottling.

"And this is our favourite wine."

Both recipes are of course better if minimum quantity of three gallons is made.

SLOE WINE

Ingredients:

3 lb. sloes
½ lb. raisins
3 lb. sugar
6 pints water
Yeast

Method:

Much the same as for elderberry. Mash the sloes well, pour over them the boiling water, and then add the minced raisins and two pounds of sugar. Stir well, cool to 70° F., add yeast, cover with a cloth, and leave to ferment in a warm room for 10 days. Then strain on to remaining sugar and pour into fermenting jar. Thereafter, continue as for elderberry. If the wine towards the end of the fermentation is a little too bitter, as it may be, a little more sugar can be added, 4 oz. at a time. Usually two such additions will produce a medium wine. The remarks about colour loss and

maturing time apply equally to sloe as to elderberry. A blend of two-thirds elderberry, one-third sloe is, I find, usually about right, if the above recipes are used, but each is an excellent wine in its own right.

TABLE WINE
(Red, Dry)
(by P. Duncan and B. Acton)

Ingredients:

12 lb. elderberries or 3½ lb. dried elderberries
6 lb. raisins
Yeast nutrient
8 lb. sugar
Acid as required (preferably 1/3rd malic, 1/3rd citric, 1/3rd tartaric mixture
Grey Owl Pommard yeast
Water up to 4½ gallons

Method:

Crush elderberries and chop raisins and add 3 gallons cold water plus one Campden tablet per gallon. After 24 hours add yeast nutrient and an actively fermenting yeast starter. Ferment on pulp for a further two days, stirring pulp into the must twice daily, then strain off the pulp and press lightly. Add all the sugar in the form of syrup and make up total quantity to 4½ gallons with water and adjust acidity to 4.0 parts per thousand (in terms of sulphuric acid). Ferment to dryness and rack into a cask. Rack initially four months later and then as required by cask conditions. The wine should remain in cask for 15–18 months, after which it it can be bottled and should remain in bottle for 12 months before consumption. It should by this time have acquired a pleasant character possibly reminiscent of a Burgundy, with an alcohol content of 12½% by volume.

TANGERINE WINE

Ingredients:

12–15 tangerines | **1 gallon water**
3 lb. sugar | **Yeast**

Method:

Peel the tangerines and crush them by hand. Discard the peel. Pour the boiling water over the crushed fruit, and leave it to soak for 12 hours. Strain, and warm the juice to assist the sugar to dissolve. Pour the juice over the sugar and stir until all the sugar is dissolved. Cool to 70° F. and add the yeast (a wine yeast or a level teaspoon of granulated yeast). Pour into fermentation jar and fit trap. Ferment until finished and the wine is clear; then rack into clean bottles. A lovely delicate wine.

"If my wife knew I had as much as this, she'd have half the village down here, sampling . . ."

TANSY WINE

(Tanacetum vulgare)

Ingredients:

1 small packet Tansy Herb
4 lb. parsnips
3½ lb. sugar
½ oz. citric acid (or 3 lemons, no pith, in lieu)
½ pint cold strong tea (or a pinch of grape tannin)
Sufficient water to produce 1 gallon must
Yeast nutrient and activated wine yeast

Method:

Clean by scrubbing the parsnips, then slice thinly and boil until just tender, but not mushy, otherwise the wine will not fall bright. Strain the liquid on to the sugar and stir until dissolved. Next pour boiling water over the tansy herb

and infuse as making tea. When cool add the tansy infusion, citric acid and cold tea to the sweetened parsnip extract. Add the yeast nutrient and activated wine yeast and ferment under an air lock in the normal way. The tansy herb should be used sparingly as it is rather hot yet at the same time pleasant and aromatic, and is used often in lieu of ginger.

GREEN TOMATO WINE
(by C. Shave)

Ingredients:

4 lb. green tomatoes
1 quart balm leaves including stalks
1 lb. raisins, sultanas or currants
1 lb. maize, barley or wheat
2 lemons or oranges (½ oz. citric acid may be used in lieu)
3 lb. sugar
1 gallon water
½ pint cold tea
Activated yeast and nutrient

Method:

Soak the grains overnight. Scald the dried fruit and pass the grains, leaves and stalks together with the tomatoes, dried fruit and fruit rinds (no white pith) through a mincer. Place the minced ingredients in the fermenting jar and add the sugar. Pour boiling water over this and stir well to dissolve the sugar. When cool add the cold tea, fruit juices or citric acid, activated yeast and nutrient. Ferment for seven days then strain into glass jars. Fit air lock, ferment and rack in the normal way.

WHEAT
(see Barley)

WHEAT AND ORANGE

WHEAT AND PRUNE
(see under Prune)

YARROW WINE
(Achillea-Millefolium)

Also known as Milfoil, the Yarrow is a weed found in pastures, roadside wastes, and on commons. In winemaking the flowers and bruised leaves (no stalk) are used. The yarrow flowers from June to the end of the year.

Ingredients:

1 gallon yarrow flowers and bruised leaves
1 lb. chopped raisins
2½ lb. sugar
½ pint cold tea
2 oranges
2 lemons (or ½ oz. citric acid)
1 gallon water
Activated yeast and nutrient

Method:

Remove the blooms and put them into a bowl with the chopped raisins; pour the boiling water over them, and leave to soak for four or five days, then strain into a pan and add the thinly peeled skins of the oranges (no white pith) and the sugar, and simmer for 20 minutes. Add the juice of the oranges and lemons (or ½ oz. citric acid) and the tea; stir, then strain immediately into a bowl or polythene bucket and allow to cool to 70° F. Add yeast and nutrient, keep well covered in a warm place for 7 days, until the first vigorous ferment has died down, then transfer to a fermenting jar and fit a fermentation lock. Wait until all fermentation has ceased —usually about two months—then rack for the first time. A second racking two or three months later will be beneficial if a second yeast deposit forms, and this time your yarrow wine can be bottled. Keep it at least six months before you drink it.

"I can't understand it—he hasn't touched his beer yet!"

"The wife won't have it made in anything else."

INDEX

INDEX

INDEX